This may be one of the most important books you can read for improving your company's performance

Sales & **Operations Planning** has emerged as an essential set of management tools in this age of global operations, supply chains that extend half a world away, and increasingly demanding customers. Its primary component – Executive S&OP – has rightfully been called "top management's handle on the business."

The mission of this book is to tell the busy executive what he or she needs to know about Executive S&OP. Written in clear, understandable language, this book can easily be read in the course of an evening or two – or on a plane ride from Chicago to L.A.

It answers these, and many other, questions:

.. Why is Executive S&OP so popular?

.. What are the benefits from doing it well?

.. How does it work?

.. What's the role of the president and his or her staff?

.. What kinds of companies are using Executive S&OP?

.. What's the best way to implement it?

Tom Wallace is a writer and educator specializing in sales & operations planning, sales forecasting, and demand management. Tom is a distinguished fellow of The Ohio State University's Center for Operational Excellence, and currently writes and speaks in conjunction with the Institute of Business Forecasting. He is the author of twelve books, including Sales & Operations Planning: The How-To Handbook.

Bob Stahl has spent the last 30 years as a practitioner and consultant developing leading edge processes for manufacturing, logistics, and supply chain management. He is a teacher, writer, and consultant with an extremely strong track record of success. Bob has worked with many of the world's leading corporations and is the co-author of Building to Customer Demand, Sales Forecasting: A New Approach, Sales & Operations Planning: The Self-Audit Workbook, and Master Scheduling in the 21st Century.

For more information on the TF Wallace Company, visit us at:

http://www.steelwedge.com/education

Steelwedge
3875 Hopyard Road, Suite 300
Pleasanton, CA 94588
925-460-1700; x 1755

Steelwedge
Plan Ready

D1221672

Sales & Operations Planning
The Executive's Guide

Also by Tom Wallace and Bob Stahl

Books:

Sales & Operations Planning: The How-To Handbook, 3rd Ed.

Sales & Operations Planning: The Self-Audit Workbook, 2nd Ed.

Building to Customer Demand

Sales Forecasting: A New Approach

Master Scheduling in the 21ˢᵗ Century

Videos/DVDs

The Executive S&OP Briefing:
A Visual Introduction by Tom Wallace

Building to Customer Demand by Tom Wallace and Bob Stahl

Procurement in the New World of Manufacturing by Bob Stahl

SALES & OPERATIONS PLANNING
THE EXECUTIVE'S GUIDE

Balancing Demand and

Supply Aligning Units and

$$$ Enhancing Teamwork

Thomas F. Wallace
&
Robert A. Stahl

T. F. Wallace & Company
2006

First Printing: September, 2006
Second Printing: February, 2007: page re-layout, minor text changes
Third Printing: October, 2008
Fourth Printing: March, 2010
Fifth Printing: May, 2011
Sixth Printing: December, 2012
Seventh Printing: September, 2014

International Standard Book Number
(ISBN): 978-0-9978877-9-2

Printed in the United States of America

This and other books and videos by Tom Wallace and/or Bob Stahl may be ordered from:

www.tfwallace.com
T.F. Wallace & Company
513-281-0500

Bob Stahl may be reached at: RStahlSr@aol.com
R. A. Stahl Company
508-226-0477

Contents

List of Figures

Acknowledgments

Thanks a million to those who reviewed this book: John Dix, Business Development Index; Phil Dolci, Sanford/Sharpie; Jim Fitterling, Dow Chemical; John Jordan, Graco; Roger Lindgren and Adam Szczepanski, V&M Star; Stijn Vande Velde, Deceuninck North America, and last but not least to our very good friend, Arvil Sexton.

Additionally we'd like to thank the superb team of people who have supported the development of this and prior books: Kim Nir – Copy Edit, David Mill – Cover Design, Kathryn Wallace – Page Layout, and Tonia Lawson at Malloy Printing. It's a true pleasure working with you.

Dedication

We dedicate this book to all of the executives, in many different companies, with whom we've worked over the years in making successful Executive S&OP a reality in their companies . . .

to Jim and Ross; Leo, Gary and Lynda; Ed and Rocco; John; Bing and Bill; Ken; Ove, Jackie, and Tim; Bill and Galen; John and Bill; Andy and Dennis; Mike and Ken; James and Pat; Bill and Jim; Doug and George; Dick and Jack; John and Joe; Lenny and Debbie; George and Don; Ray; Mike and Rhetta; Tom and Sherryl; Maggie and Paul; Ken and Brad; Bill and Jim; Marcello; Jim, Pat, and Doug; Cathy and Jacqueline; Lach, Jeff, and Scott; Don and Joe; Stacey and Jim; Bob and Carl; Dan, Gene, and Brian; Jack and Mike; Scott and Mike; Bernie; Dave, Ed, and Gary; Jeff; Jim and Dave; John, Kristie, and Laurel; Howard, John, and Marta; Dave and Tom; Howard, Phil, Darryl, Dean, and Bill; Dave; Rhoda; Bob and Bill; Syd and John; Al; Dave and Brent; Tony and Bob; Dick, Marc, and Paul; John, Chris, and Tony; Ron and Jamie; Tom and Ken; Roger, Adam, and Amy; Mike and Sue; Chris and Joe; Tony and Bob, and others . . . .

We're honored to have worked with you.

Preface: A Terminology Issue

The term Sales & Operations Planning traditionally referred to a decision-making process for balancing demand and supply in *aggregate*. This is an executive-centered activity.

However, in the recent past, common usage of this term has broadened to include tools and techniques that operate at a lower, more *detailed* level, for individual products and customer orders. These are not executive-centered processes; they carry too much detail.

In this book, we use the term *Executive S&OP* to refer to the executive activity. We use *Sales & Operations Planning* to refer to the larger set of processes, which include the processes for forecasting and planning at the detail level as well as Executive S&OP. The only stand-alone use of the acronym *S&OP* will be in conjunction with spreadsheets and software.

Appendix A contains further details.

Introduction

We queried a handful of executives whose companies are successful users of Executive S&OP in order to get their reactions to the process. Some of their quotes are on the back panel of the dust jacket. Others follow.

On Decision Making

Executive S&OP has put more discipline and transparency into the process than it may have had historically. This takes some of the "emotion" out of the decision making process and makes it more fact based. We are making these decisions weeks and months ahead of time, instead of days and weeks ahead of time.

> Jim Fitterling
> Global Business Vice President
> Dow Chemical Company

Addressing long-term issues was always ad hoc, based on someone analyzing an issue and being able to get it on a management meeting agenda. Now we have a comprehensive scan of our demand and production future up to 18 months, which captures critical issues. At last week's Executive S&OP meeting [May 2006], we launched a project team to study a supply challenge . . . expected in September 2007.

> Adam Szczepanski
> CFO
> V&M Star
> Division of Vallourec & Mannesmann

On Teamwork

Executive S&OP has increased the level of teamwork and communication within the company. There is a lot less of the "us" versus "them" mentality.

> Phil Dolci
> Vice President and General Manager
> Sanford/Sharpie
> Division of Newell-Rubbermaid

Executive S&OP has become a very powerful communication tool. Much of the necessary information was in silos before and, when shared, it may have been too late to react. Now the whole team knows all.

> Roger Lindgren
> President & CEO
> V&M Star
> Division of Vallourec & Mannesmann

Executive S&OP streamlined the communication flow throughout the organization and created a forum for debate and ultimately agreement. Communication between Planning, Sales, and Marketing has improved dramatically along with a consistent forward vision.

> John Jordan
> CFO
> Graco Children's Products
> Division of Newell-Rubbermaid

On Financial Planning, Budgeting, and Reporting

The financial plan in Executive S&OP is "the plan" so when we need updated forecasts and production plans as the basis for the coming year's business plan, we already have them. There is no need to ask for what we plan to sell and produce, so we just focus on refinements such as operating expenses.

Adam Szczepanski, CFO

Sarbanes-Oxley has taken away our ability to manage the results, so predicting the impact of sales and supply performance on a quarterly basis is critical in maintaining integrity with the Street. Executive S&OP is a big help with this.

John Jordan, CFO

You may have noticed that none of these executives are talking about the quantifiable benefits that traditionally come from Executive S&OP: higher customer service levels, lower inventories, more stable production rates, and so forth. Does that mean they're not getting these benefits?

Not at all. As a group, they reported sizeable improvements in customer service, inventory turns, production rate stability, and obsolescence. In the coming chapters, we'll talk about both S&OP's hard, quantifiable benefits as well as the softer kinds of benefits cited above. Stay tuned.

Chapter 1

Why All the Buzz About
Sales & Operations Planning?

Let's eavesdrop on an executive staff meeting at the Acme Widget Company, an imaginary manufacturer of widgets for home and industry.

President: *This shortage situation is terrible. When will we ever get our act together? Whenever business gets good, we run out of product and our customer service is lousy.*

VP Operations: *I'll tell you when. When we start to get some decent forecasts from Sales & Marketing.*

VP Sales & Marketing (interrupting): *Wait a minute. We forecasted this upturn.*

VP Operations: *Yeah, but not in time to do anything about it. We got the revised forecast four days after the start of the month. By then it was too late.*

VP Sales & Marketing: *I could have told you months ago. All you had to do was ask.*

VP Finance: *I'd like to be in on those conversations. We've been burned more than once by building inventories for a business upturn that doesn't happen. Then we get stuck with tons of inventory and run out of cash.*

President: *As the warden said to Paul Newman in* Cool Hand Luke, *"What we have here is a failure to communicate." We just have to do a better job of keeping each other up to date.*

And the beat goes on: back orders, dissatisfied customers, high inventories, late shipments, finger pointing, cash-flow problems, demand and supply out of balance, missing the business plan. This is the norm in many companies.

It does not have to be that way. Today a large and growing number of companies are using a business process called Executive S&OP to help avoid these kinds of problems. We think there are four main reasons for its popularity:

1. Companies are reporting substantial benefits from Executive S&OP, and the word gets around. Sizeable gains in customer service levels, decreases in inventory, more stable production rates, and more controlled and rapid new product launches are significant benefits – and there are many more.

2. Complexity and the rate of change are both increasing. Let's tackle complexity first:

   a. Businesses are becoming more global. Managing operations around the world is a greater challenge; it increases the complexity factor by an order of magnitude.

   b. Supply chains are lengthening and hence becoming harder to manage. Executive S&OP helps people to balance demand and supply not only inside the company but also externally – to the customers, suppliers, contract manufacturers, transportation resources and so forth – perhaps half a world away.

   c. Regarding rate of change, this is the first decade of the twenty-first century. Not much more needs to be said.

Consumers are becoming ever more demanding; product life cycles are shortening; and sourcing is moving all over the globe. And then moving again. And again.

3. The Lean Manufacturing community is discovering Executive S&OP. As product life cycles shorten and as demand becomes ever more volatile, many successful Lean companies are turning to Executive S&OP to help them better project future demand and harmonize it with supply, even though Executive S&OP was not invented as a part of Lean Manufacturing.

4. Executive S&OP's time has come, based on what we call the *adoption curve* for new processes.

Let's look at each of these reasons in greater detail.

1. Benefits from Executive S&OP

Companies doing a first-rate job of Executive S&OP cite benefits in two main categories, the first being *hard* benefits – those that can be readily measured and assigned a financial impact. These include:

- Higher customer service: the ability to ship on time virtually all the time. This results from Executive S&OP's ability to help people balance future demand and supply, so that *current* demand and supply are in balance.

- Lower finished goods inventories, simultaneously with the increases in customer service just mentioned. Executive S&OP enables a company's managers to set the desired level of finished inventory, and then to manage the business proactively to achieve those levels.

- More stable supply rates, resulting in higher productivity for the plants, the suppliers, and contract manufacturers. Because Executive S&OP is forward-looking, it helps people make changes to supply rates *earlier* and in *smaller* increments.

- Faster and more controlled new product launches. Here also, because of Executive S&OP's forward-looking orientation, potential problems – for example with plant capacities, supplier capacities, product availability for tests and samples, and so forth – can be seen *early*, with sufficient time to remove those potential obstacles before they become real ones.

- Shorter customer order backlogs, hence shorter lead times, for companies whose business is primarily make-to-order. As with the finished inventory, the order backlog – all customer orders in house but not yet shipped – can be targeted and managed proactively to achieve the desired levels.

These are solid benefits but they're not all of the good things that result. The other category is *soft* benefits, and they can be substantial:

- Enhanced teamwork within the executive team and within the operating levels of the business. Executive S&OP was "invented" at the U. S. Pharmaceutical Division of Abbott Labs. The division president, a man named Milt, said that with this process, "Marketing can challenge Production proposals, Finance can question advertising concepts, and all disciplines participate in the finalization of the production rate proposed by Materials Management. My goal is to get everyone seeing the business through my glasses."[1] That means seeing the business more holistically, with less of a silo effect.

- Better decisions with less effort and time, yielding better results. We see parallel results in the world of physical products: better production and quality processes yield higher quality products – at *lower* cost, not higher. In an Executive S&OP context, better *decision-making* processes yield better decisions – with *less* effort and time, not more.

- Improved financial plans with less effort and time, and which are aligned with the operational plans. During the implementation of Executive S&OP at a wire and cable company, the CEO – a guy named Steve – said: "One of the benefits we expect to get from this process is to reduce sharply the amount of time we have to spend each year doing the financial plan and budget. We can't afford to have our important people tied up with that for weeks on end; their job is to design products, market and sell products, produce products, and get them distributed."

- Greater accountability for results. Executive S&OP puts a spotlight on accountability. That's a solid benefit, but it may make the implementation process more difficult. More on this in Chapter 7, which deals with implementation.

- Better control of the business through the use of one, agreed-upon set of numbers. With Executive S&OP, no longer does

---

[1] "Game Planning," by David Rucinski. *Production and Inventory Management Journal*, First Quarter 1982, pp. 63–68.

Marketing have its own forecast, which differs from the forecast that Sales has, which in turn is different from the one Operations is using and, of course, none of these three agree with the forecast being used in Finance. Executive S&OP, done properly, results in one set of numbers – in units and dollars – with which to run the business.[2]

- A window into the future, by being able to see potential problems soon enough to prevent them from becoming actual problems. It's uncanny, but Executive S&OP does enable people to see farther and more clearly into the future – and thus avoid the obstacles, pitfalls, and so forth that lurk out there.

Considering all of these benefits – hard and soft – it's easy to see why Executive S&OP is called "top management's handle on the business." An example: following an Executive S&OP meeting where some very major decisions were made, the CEO said to one of your authors, "Tom, when I think back to a year ago, before we had this process, I wonder how we ran the business without it."

The word gets around, and also people get around. For example, the president of Division A – a lady named Maggie – led a successful Executive S&OP process in her division. Upon being promoted to head up Division B, she is now involved in implementing it there. She took it with her. Another example: John, the COO at Company D, became the CEO at Company F; he

---

[2] Many publicly traded companies follow the principle of "underpromise and overdeliver." They'll use two sets of numbers: one for the financial community, containing plans expected to be attained, and one for internal purposes with stretch goals, which may or may not be completely achieved. That's fine. They run with one set of *internal* numbers – the stretch goals – and that's what we're talking about here.

took Executive S&OP with him into his new company because he had such a positive experience with it at his prior company. These are not infrequent occurrences.

2. Complexity and the Rate of Change

Do you need Executive S&OP in your company? It depends. If your business is very simple and stable, maybe not. If you have a small and contented customer base, few products, and short lead times, and if things rarely change, you can probably do all of the forward planning necessary on the back of an envelope. Seen many companies like that lately?

Let's take a look at Figure 1-1, on the next page. It says that as complexity and the rate of change increase or decrease, the need for Sales & Operations Planning, including its executive component, increases or decreases right along with them.

There are countervailing forces at work here. Lean Manufacturing, which we'll get into in just a moment, will push a company *down* the diagonal, towards more simplicity. Pushing upward are two factors: global operations – selling and producing product around the world – and extended supply chains – sourcing products and/or components from half a world away.

For many companies, this nets out to more complexity, not less. Thus they need more robust tools to coordinate these global operations and extended supply chains. Many companies have turned to Executive S&OP to provide that robust coordination needed today.

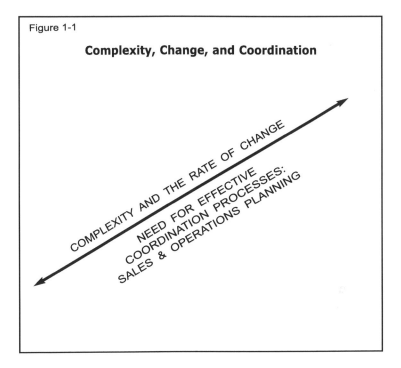

Figure 1-1

Complexity, Change, and Coordination

COMPLEXITY AND THE RATE OF CHANGE
NEED FOR EFFECTIVE
COORDINATION PROCESSES:
SALES & OPERATIONS PLANNING

3. Lean Manufacturing and Executive S&OP

You might be thinking, well why can't Lean Manufacturing simplify things enough so that Executive S&OP is not needed?

In some cases, perhaps it can. Lean's task, among others, is to simplify, speed up, and eliminate waste. It does this best in those operations over which it has a high degree of leverage: primarily the plants and suppliers. Toyota is the poster child for Lean Manufacturing, and it is arguably the best manufacturing company in the world.

For many companies, the leverage over customers is often weak to nonexistent, certainly much less than with one's own plants and suppliers. Demand is variable. It can ebb and flow, and that can give Lean a problem. Why? Because Lean thrives on linearity and stability. Lean dislikes variability and, most of all, variability of demand. It simply doesn't work as well with variable demand.

So the question arises: how does Toyota handle this? Well, at the risk of sounding sacrilegious, we must point out that Toyota's *total* supply chain is not particularly Lean. It certainly is in the Toyota plants and at the suppliers. It's at the distribution and retail end of Toyota's supply chain where Lean goes away.

Toyota produces vehicles in a very Lean, linear fashion and then, when they come off the assembly line, it "pushes" them into a huge finished goods inventory estimated conservatively to range from $2 to $3 billion: the dealer inventory in the field.[3] This serves as a shock absorber for variations in demand, and thus Toyota manufacturing is insulated from the ups and downs of demand by the end consumers; it can change production rates gradually and thereby minimize disruptions.

Many companies implement Lean Manufacturing but don't have the luxury of such a large finished goods inventory. They follow the Toyota model because it's the most prominent in the Lean literature and because many of the Lean consultants active today learned their Lean while working at Toyota or from those who did. As the initial parts of Lean are implemented in these kinds of companies, they take to heart the Lean principle of continuous improvement. They work hard at making it better. And, at some point, someone raises the question: "Rather than getting surprised so often, wouldn't it be nice if we could see the demand shifts

---

[3] To Toyota's credit, its inventory of vehicles in the field is substantially lower, based on days' supply, than many of their competitors. But the fact remains that it's huge.

sooner, and get our production rates harmonized gradually with the new demand that's coming?"

That's called balancing demand and supply, and that's where Executive S&OP lives.

4. Executive S&OP's Time Has Come

There seems to be about a 20-year lag between the invention of a new business process and its widespread adoption. Think about it:

- Manufacturing Resource Planning/Enterprise Resource Planning was invented back in the 1960s but didn't really kick in until the '80s. Yes, there was a blip around the turn of the century, with Y2K, but that was primarily a software issue and much less focused on process.

- Total Quality/Six Sigma was around for a long time before it got popular during the late 1980s. For quite some time, everybody was "doing TQM." Then its adoption rate leveled off and today the TQM/Six Sigma tools and processes are an accepted feature of the business landscape.

- Just-In-Time/Lean Manufacturing came over from Japan in the 1970s but didn't get big until the mid- to late-'90s – for reasons we couldn't figure out. "This stuff is so good," we kept saying, "why isn't everybody doing it? What's the matter with our manufacturing industry?"

We call this lag the *adoption curve for new processes* and it's depicted in Figure 1-2. Executive S&OP was invented in the early

1980s and didn't start to get very popular until a few years ago. You can see in the figure that we're predicting that Executive S&OP still has a way to run, and then will level off in rate of adoption and become – as with the others – one of the widely used tools in the management tool kit.

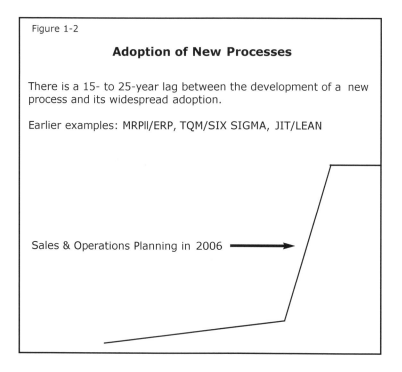

Figure 1-2

Adoption of New Processes

There is a 15- to 25-year lag between the development of a new process and its widespread adoption.

Earlier examples: MRPII/ERP, TQM/SIX SIGMA, JIT/LEAN

Sales & Operations Planning in 2006

FAQ (Frequently Asked Questions): *About those benefits you mentioned, do all companies get all of the benefits?*

Some companies get *all* the hard benefits. Most companies get *most* of them. Some companies, mostly those doing a lot of the right things already, get *some* of the hard benefits. It's a bit like a bell-shaped curve.

Regarding the soft benefits – enhanced teamwork, better decisions, window into the future, and so forth – virtually all companies get all of these.

This answer, of course, assumes that authentic Executive S&OP was implemented well. If not, all bets are off.

And what does it cost to implement it well?

Surprisingly little, for three reasons:

- Executive S&OP involves relatively few people, perhaps several dozen or less in a business unit of average size.[4] This differs from initiatives such as Six Sigma, Lean Manufacturing, and others, which involve a high percentage of the people in the company. Therefore education and training costs for Executive S&OP are far less.

- Large amounts of consulting simply aren't necessary. All that's usually needed is periodic guidance by a professional experienced in Executive S&OP and highly skilled in dealing with top management. One to two visits per month for six to ten months should be sufficient.

- Traditionally, most companies use spreadsheet software for the collation and display of Executive S&OP information, importing the data from their main systems: ERP, CRM, legacy, and so forth. In these cases, no additional software costs are incurred. If Executive S&OP-specific software is acquired, this cost should be under $100,000.

---

[4] Annual sales volume of roughly $.5 to $1.5 billion.

The total costs of implementation for the average business shouldn't exceed several hundred thousand dollars and could be much less. As one of our CFO friends remarked about Executive S&OP: *"The costs get lost in the rounding. And the benefits are really, really big. You can't afford not to do it."*

Coming up next: Okay, it's popular. So what is it?

Chapter 2

So Just What Is Sales & Operations Planning?

Sales & Operations Planning, as used in the broad sense, is a set of decision-making processes with three main objectives:

1. To balance demand and supply

2. To align volume and mix

3. To integrate operational plans with financial plans

Let's take a look at each one.

1. Balancing Demand and Supply

All of us learned about demand and supply back in Economics 101, except our professors probably referred to it as supply and demand. Many economists still do. Unfortunately that reflects an obsolete mind-set, a carryover from the Post-World War II era when supply was short and companies could sell everything they made.

We prefer to put demand first, because that's where it should be. Demand is the driver. It's what the customers want, and today they're the boss. Supply, of course, refers to the resources one has available to meet the demand.

Is it important to have demand and supply in balance? Indeed it is. If demand exceeds supply – by more than a little bit for more than a little while – bad things can happen: stock outs,   missed shipments, unhappy customers, increased costs of purchased items, premium freight, unplanned overtime, and more.

If supply exceeds demand by more than a little bit for more than a little while, bad things can also happen: excess inventory, cash flow problems, the possibility – or reality – of a layoff, reduced production volume, and the attendant lower overhead absorption.

Now, is it always bad if demand and supply aren't in balance? No, sometimes it can be a good thing. It all depends on where the imbalance lies. For example, if projected demand ten months in the future exceeds current supply, and if the company can economically add more capacity sooner than that, that's fine. Demand is growing; business is good. Being able to see the projected imbalances soon enough is what's needed, so that the *potential* imbalance problems can be eliminated before they become *actual* problems.

One of Sales & Operations Planning's main jobs is to help people balance demand and supply.

2. Aligning Volume and Mix

Unlike demand and supply, volume and mix aren't exactly household terms. To get a handle on what they mean in this context, let's take a look at Figure 2-1.

Here are the differences between volume and mix:

- Volume is an aggregate issue – the big picture – while mix is the details.

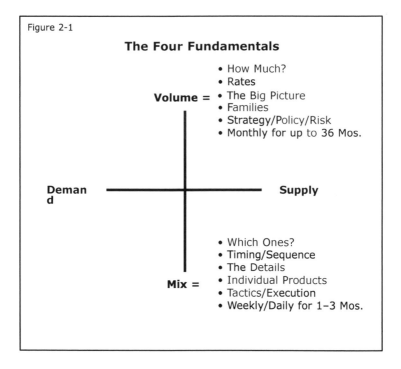

Figure 2-1

The Four Fundamentals

Volume =
- How Much?
- Rates
- The Big Picture
- Families
- Strategy/Policy/Risk
- Monthly for up to 36 Mos.

Demand ———————————— **Supply**

Mix =
- Which Ones?
- Timing/Sequence
- The Details
- Individual Products
- Tactics/Execution
- Weekly/Daily for 1–3 Mos.

• Volume is often expressed in product families or groups while mix exists at the level of individual products, stockkeeping units (SKUs), and customer orders.

• The volume question is "how much?" while mix is concerned with "which ones?" – as in "which job to run first, second, and third?" or "should we ship the Jones order on Thursday and the Smith order on Friday or vice versa?"

Questions of volume precede those of mix, so wise companies plan their volumes first, and spend enough time and effort to do it well. They find that doing so makes mix problems much less difficult. But where do most companies spend almost all of their time? On mix. Many look at volumes only once per year, when they do the Business Plan. They probably wouldn't do it even that often, except the financial folks make them do it. Once each year, the CFO says, "Well, folks, it's budget time again . . ."

So why do most companies spend more than 99 percent of their time on mix issues to the exclusion of volume? It's simple: mix – individual products – is what companies ship to their customers. That's where the pressure is. Mix is seen as important and urgent. The effective planning of future volumes may be seen as important, but it is in fact less urgent.

As a result, many companies set their volumes – sales rates and production rates – no more than once per year, when they do their annual business plan. But how often during an average year do volume needs change? It's almost always more often than once every twelve months. For most companies, it's more than once per quarter.

Just as demand is the driver of supply, so volume should be the driver of mix. (See the figure on page 19.) The volume plans, authorized by senior management, set the rates and levels of activity within which the mix activities must conform. We submit that most companies don't work hard enough at forecasting and planning their volumes and spend too much time trying to predict mix. They overwork the details and don't focus enough on the big picture.

So, another primary objective for Sales & Operations Planning is to align volume and mix – routinely.

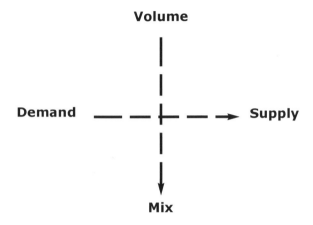

3. Integrating Operational Plans with Financial Plans

In many companies, the operational plans are not tied to the financial plans authorized by top management. Is this important? Absolutely. The operational plans drive activities in the real world: the customer order department, the receiving dock, the plant floor, and the shipping dock.

Therefore, when the operational plans deviate from the financial plans, it's likely that real-world results will not match the financial plan. But the financial plan is, in effect, top management's commitment up the line: to the corporate office, to the board, to the financial community. This is a serious shortcoming in many companies, and it is perhaps one of the reasons why the average tenure of leaders of businesses – CEOs, COOs, presidents, general managers, managing directors – is relatively short.

For almost all executives, the overarching element in business is financial performance. They're measured by it; they're compensated by it; their careers can literally live or die by it. Thus another primary objective for Executive S&OP is to integrate the operational plans with the financial plans.

So now, let's revisit the four fundamentals and see how the tools in Sales & Operations Planning support them (See Figure 2-2.)

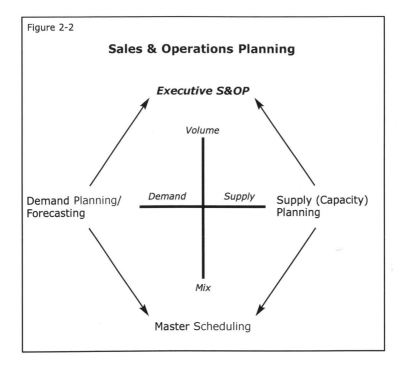

Figure 2-2

Sales & Operations Planning

Executive S&OP

Volume

Demand Planning/ Forecasting

Demand   *Supply*

Supply (Capacity) Planning

Mix

Master Scheduling

This figure is telling us that:

• The total Sales & Operations Planning set of processes operates at both the volume and mix levels. It includes:

- Executive S&OP (for volume)

- Master Scheduling (for mix)

- Demand Planning/Forecasting and Supply (Capacity) Planning, which feed both Executive S&OP and Master Scheduling

• Executive S&OP is that part of Sales & Operations Planning that deals with volumes, utilizing tools for aggregate forecasting and aggregate supply planning. This is the point of contact and control for executive management, their handle on the business. As we said in the Preface, we're using the term *Executive S&OP* when referring to the executive process and *Sales & Operations Planning* for the larger entity, which includes mix issues.[1]

• Executive S&OP:

- operates with aggregated groupings of products: product groups, product families and subfamilies, and so forth.

- occurs on a monthly cycle, with provisions for mid-cycle updates when changing conditions dictate.

- has a forward planning horizon of 15 to 36 months.

---

[1] For more on this, see the Preface on page *xv* and Appendix A.

- Master Scheduling is more detailed. This process:

  - operates with mix: individual products, SKUs, and customer orders.

  - has a time frame of days or weeks.

  - extends into the future for an amount of time necessary for production of individual products and the procurement of their components.[2] This could be extremely short, several days or less, which could be the case with companies using Lean Manufacturing effectively – or several months for products and specialized components outsourced from far away.

The Master Scheduling process gets input from Executive S&OP and from the detailed forecasting and capacity planning tools. Master Scheduling drives the even more detailed planning and scheduling tools of Plant Scheduling and Supplier Scheduling, which can be done in a traditional fashion or via Kanban (from the world of Lean Manufacturing) or by using Advanced Planning Systems (powerful algorithmic approaches to solving short-term scheduling problems). These processes can occur by day, by shift, by hour, or even less.

In addition, the Master Schedule interacts with processes for distribution center (DC) replenishment; it receives demands from the DCs and plans the availability of product for them.

---

[2] In the jargon of the trade, this is referred to as the "Planning Time Fence."

Where Sales & Operations Planning Fits

Fifty years ago, very few tools existed to help people manage their businesses better. Since then, an abundance of superb tools has been developed: Total Quality Management/Six Sigma, Just-In-Time/Lean Manufacturing, Manufacturing Resource Planning/Enterprise Resource Planning, and many others.

That's good news. The problem is that the sheer volume of these tools is a bit overwhelming. Where do these tools fit? Which tool does what?

Our colleague, Chris Gray, has a good way of simplifying this. He categorizes the tools by their mission: increase quality, reduce waste, and enhance coordination. See Figure 2-3.

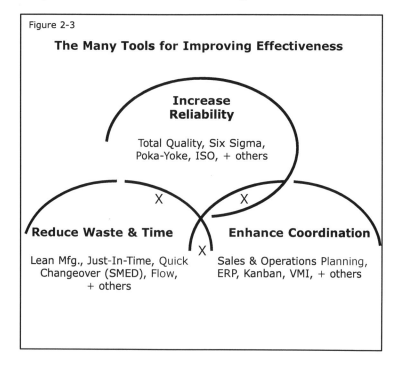

Figure 2-3

The Many Tools for Improving Effectiveness

Increase Reliability

Total Quality, Six Sigma, Poka-Yoke, ISO, + others

X   X

Reduce Waste & Time

X

Lean Mfg., Just-In-Time, Quick Changeover (SMED), Flow, + others

Enhance Coordination

Sales & Operations Planning, ERP, Kanban, VMI, + others

Here we can see that the mission of Six Sigma is to increase quality, that Lean Manufacturing's job is to reduce waste and time, and that Sales & Operations Planning is primarily a tool to enhance coordination. And of course, the Xs in the diagram show that there's overlap among the three toolsets: if you increase quality, you'll reduce waste – and so on.

"Connecting the Knobs"

The vice president and general manager of a $2 billion per year consumer goods business had an interesting way of putting it. He said, "Before we had Executive S&OP in the company, I spent a lot of my time *turning knobs that weren't connected to anything*."

What he was saying is that the decisions he made at his level may or may not get transmitted down to affect directly what happens in the customer order department or on the plant floor, the receiving dock, and most important of all, the shipping dock. Or, if they did get communicated, they might get garbled on the way down. Or two or more other things might get messed up in the process. There was a disconnect in the process. See the left side of Figure 2-4.

He went on to say, "This process connects the knobs." Executive S&OP links the top level strategic and financial plans of the business to the week-to-week, day-to-day, or shift-to-shift activities of acquiring material, converting it into finished product, and shipping it to customers.

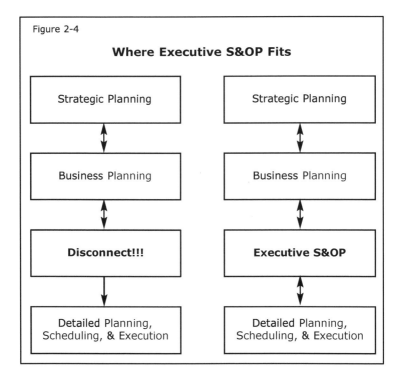

Figure 2-4

Where Executive S&OP Fits

FAQ: *Why shouldn't Executive S&OP work with mix instead of volume? After all, mix is specific products – it's what we ship out the back door. That sounds more important.*

This question gets to the heart of what Executive S&OP is and is not. It is most definitely not a short-run scheduling and expediting tool. Rather, it's a medium- to long-range planning process; it's directional, not detailed. Remember, volume drives mix just as demand drives supply.

In addition to that, here's a more specific reason: executives simply don't have the time or the desire to get involved in large amounts of detail. And they shouldn't have to. That's not their job. That's the job of people who work in places called Planning, Supply Chain, Logistics, Purchasing, and so on.

A third reason: for medium- to long-range planning – months 2 or 3 through months 15 to 18 – it's possible to generate detailed demand and supply plans that far into the future, look at them, approve them, and then sum them up into aggregate numbers. The problem is that this is almost always *less accurate* and *more work* than projecting the aggregate numbers into the future. The aggregate numbers can then be used to derive whatever detail is needed – and that normally isn't much.

Coming up in the next chapter: a sad, twisted tale entitled "Bad Day at Acme Widget."

Chapter 3

Bad Day at Acme Widget

Two important elements of Executive S&OP are: 1) the manner in which the information is displayed and 2) and a defined process for decision making. First, we'll look at the display issue.

Let's revisit the Acme Widget Company, which we first saw back in Chapter 1. Here, Mike Marshall, a product manager at Acme, is doing his quarterly review of the forecasts for his products. He's looking at a display for the Medium Consumer Widget family. (The numbers on this and the following pages are in thousands.)

	FEB	MAR	APR	MAY	JUN	JUL	AUG
FORECAST	100	100	100	100	120	120	120
ACTUAL SALES	90	95	85				
DIFFERENCE	−10	−5	−15				
CUM DIFFERENCE		−15	−30				

Mike is concerned that sales are consistently below what he's forecasted. Over the last three months, actual sales have been 10 percent less than forecast. Mike scratches his head, checks a couple of reports he recently received from field salespeople, and concludes that this product family is losing business to another family that the company recently introduced. He decides to revise the forecast downward and, with a few quick strokes on his computer keyboard, does so.

	FEB	MAR	APR		MAY	JUN	JUL	AUG
FORECAST	100	100	100	OLD	100	120	120	120
				NEW	90	90	90	90
ACTUAL SALES	90	95	85					
DIFFERENCE	−10	−5	15					
CUM DIFFERENCE		−15	30					

Mike has reduced his forecast by 10,000 per month in May and by 30,000 per month after that, thereby wiping out the forecast increase that he had made for June and beyond. Remembering a conversation he had recently with Carol Clark, the chief financial officer, about high inventories, he decides to notify the plant of the forecast change. He sends Pete Prentice, the plant manager, an e-mail containing the spreadsheet with the new forecast.

Pete reacts to the e-mail message by checking his production plan for Medium Consumer Widgets:

	FEB	MAR	APR	MAY	JUN	JUL	AUG
PLANNED PRODUCTION	100	100	100	110	120	120	120
ACTUAL PRODUCTION	98	100	101				
DIFFERENCE	−2	—	+1				
CUM DIFFERENCE	−2	−2	−1				

Pete scratches his head and thinks to himself, *Man, this is a double whammy. Not only is he dropping the forecast, he's taking out the increase set for June. And we're already ramping up to 120,000 per month. Nuts!* Pete calls Mike; they talk a bit, and Pete concludes there's no choice but to cut production back. He lays out a new plan, recognizing that there's not much he can do to cut back the May output, since the month is already more than half over:

	FEB	MAR	APR		MAY	JUN	JUL	AUG
PLANNED PRDN	100	100	100	OLD	110	120	120	120
				NEW	110	100	100	90
ACTUAL PRDN	98	100	101					
DIFFERENCE	−2	—	+1					
CUM DIFFERENCE		−2	−1					

Meanwhile, back in the Finance department Carol Collins, the CFO, has just finished a rather difficult phone call with the company's banker. It centered on such things as excess inventories, negative cash flow, and the need to increase the line of credit. Carol promised the banker that she personally would dig into these problems and get them fixed.

She takes a look at her finished goods inventory report and soon comes across the page for Medium Consumer Widgets:

		FEB	MAR	APR	MAY	JUN	JUL	AUG
PLANNED INVENTORY (1-MO SUPPLY)		100	100	100	110	120	120	120
ACTUAL INV	103	111	116	132				
DIFFERENCE		+3	+11	+16	+32			

Carol's concerned about the inventory build-up on Medium Consumer Widgets. They now have 132,000 units in stock, which is much higher than the budgeted one-month supply. At a standard cost of $50 each, that's $1,600,000 over plan.

She calls Pete at the plant: "Pete, the inventory of Medium Widgets is way up there – 30 percent above authorized. Are you guys working on bringing that down? If so, can I count on the inventory starting to drop?"

Pete replies, "Carol, we're aware of the problem. The bad news is that it's a lot worse than your numbers are showing." He tells her about Mike's downward forecast revision, and they arrange to meet that afternoon. Later, at their meeting, Pete shows Carol Mike's new forecast and his new production plan.

Mike's Forecast:

	FEB	MAR	APR		MAY	JUN	JUL	AUG
FORECAST	100	100	100	NEW FCST	90	90	90	90
ACTUAL SALES	90	95	85					
DIFFERENCE	−10	−5	15					
CUM DIFFERENCE		−15	30					

Pete's Production Plan:

	FEB	MAR	APR		MAY	JUN	JUL	AUG
PLANNED PRDN	100	100	100	NEW PLAN	110	100	100	90
ACTUAL	98	100	101					
DIFFERENCE	−2	—	+1					
CUM DIFFERENCE		−2	1					

Carol, fearing the worst, picks up a pencil and calculates the projected inventory out into the future. She does this by starting with the 132 finished inventory balance at the end of April, subtracting the sales forecast for each month, and adding in Pete's planned production. Here's what she comes up with:

	APR	*MAY*	*JUN*	*JUL*	*AUG*
INVENTORY	*132*	*152*	*162*	*172*	*172*

"Good grief!" is Carol's response. "This is awful. The inventory's going over 170,000 − and staying there! That's almost twice as much as we need. At $50 each, we're going to have $8½ million tied up in Medium Widgets. Our budget for all finished goods is $10 million. What's going on here?"

"Hey, don't blame me," counters Pete. "I just got the new forecast this morning. Seems to me they should have called those numbers down months ago. I've been saying for a long time that the product managers don't look at the forecasts often enough."

Carol: "Pete, I'm afraid you'll need to cut production back a lot more than what you've got here. We just can't live with that inventory."

Pete: "Well, if we gotta then we gotta. But that means either a layoff or a plant shut-down, which not only costs money but will really drag down morale. And when morale goes down, so does productivity. If we do this, there's no way we can make our numbers for the year."

Carol: "I'll get this on the agenda for Monday's executive staff meeting and we can present the issue then. In the meantime, I'll touch base with Mike to see if maybe they can do something to jack up sales."

So, we can conclude that operating level managers at Acme also have a communications problem – not just the executives as we saw in Chapter 1. In our experience, this is almost always the case; problems such as this are not confined to only one tier of management.

What's Wrong with This Picture?

A lot. Here's some constructive criticism to Mike, Pete, and Carol:

- Mike's not reviewing his forecasts frequently enough. A once-per-quarter review simply isn't adequate for most businesses; they're too fast-paced, too dynamic, too subject to change.

- As a result, demand and supply have become way out of balance. Pete, the plant manager, is faced with a severe cutback in output rates and a likely layoff.

- The activities are disconnected. Each person is looking at his or her part of the business, but nowhere is the entire picture being brought together. The CFO, Carol, is in this particular loop mainly because the bank has been hassling her.

- The problem is sufficiently serious that Carol will escalate it to the executive staff meeting. This will most likely consume a fair amount of time, be a difficult discussion, and include some finger-pointing and fault-finding. It will not tend to enhance teamwork among the top management team.

Bottom line: these folks lack a process to routinely review the status of demand and supply, and to make timely, informed decisions about keeping them in balance. What's lacking at Acme Widget is an Executive S&OP process.

A Better Way to Look at It

Let's pretend for a moment that Acme was just beginning to implement Executive S&OP. Sally Smith, the sales administration manager, is heading up the implementation project and she has just put together an S&OP spreadsheet for Medium Consumer Widgets, a make-to-stock product family.

The following page shows a highly simplified version of what that spreadsheet might look like.

	FEB	MAR	APR	MAY	JUN	JUL	AUG
FORECAST	100	100	100	100	120	120	120
ACTUAL SALES	90	95	85				
DIFFERENCE	−10	−5	−15				
CUM DIFF	−15	−30					
PLANNED PRDN	100	100	100	110	120	120	120
ACTUAL PRDN	98	100	101				
DIFFERENCE	−2	—	+1				
CUM DIFFERENCE		−2	−1				
PLANNED INV	100	100	100	142	142	142	142
ACTUAL INV 103	111	116	132				
DIFFERENCE	+11	+16	+32				

Let's examine this display for a moment. Notice how both the demand and supply numbers are shown adjacent to each other. They're followed by the inventory projection, which in effect is the critique of the demand/supply relationship.

The result is a holistic picture of the product family's demand and supply balance. This kind of display contains information specific to each of the three key functions:

- forecasts and actual sales performance for Sales and Marketing,

- the production plan and performance to it for Operations, and

- the inventory status and outlook for the people in Finance, among others.

Each function can view not only its own numbers but also those from other areas. That makes it much easier for managers from a variety of functions to view the business as an organic whole, rather than looking only at their part of it. In the example on the previous page, we can see the inventory growth far above plan.

We can also get back to the cause: actual sales below forecast. If Sally Smith and her colleagues at Acme Widget had been looking at these numbers every month, they would have been able to *take action sooner* – and not have had to deal with such a major problem as the one they're now facing.

You've just seen the underlying logic of Executive S&OP and how the results are displayed. Granted, this is a quite simplified example, but it's the basis for virtually all S&OP displays regardless of whether they're used for product families that are:

- make-to-stock (with finished goods inventory),

- make-to-order (with no finished inventories but with customer order backlogs),

- finish-to-order (with neither finished inventories nor backlogs of any size, but with an inventory of semi-finished products awaiting receipt of the customer order and finishing).[1]

At the beginning of this chapter, we said that two important elements of Executive S&OP are: 1) the display of information and 2) a defined process for decision making. We've discussed the first one, the display, and in the next chapter we'll tackle the process for decision making.

---

[1] Finish-to-order is also referred to as assemble-to-order, blend-to-order, package-to-order, and – in the case of Dell Computer – build-to-order.

FAQ: *Do most companies use graphical or tabular displays for their Executive meetings?*

The answer is yes – they tend to use both. Graphical displays have the advantage of being much better at showing relationships and being easier to view. They're clearer and more "viewer friendly." On the other hand, tabular displays can include a good bit more information and sometimes that's necessary to support decision making.

Most companies will use graphs as the primary medium, and back up each one with a tabular display should the discussion require a closer look at some of the numbers. The tabular displays are shown only as needed.

Chapter 4

The Five-Step Process

The essence of Executive S&OP is decision making. For each product family, a decision is made on the basis of recent history, recommendations from middle management, and the executive team's knowledge of business conditions. The decision can be:

- Change the Sales Plan.

- Change the Operations Plan.

- Change the inventory/backlog projection.

- None of the above: the current plans are okay.

These decisions form the authorized plans by the president, all involved vice presidents, and others on the executive team: the overall game plan for Sales, Operations, Finance, and Product Development. (New product plans are reviewed for their needs and their impact on the demand and supply picture.)

Executive S&OP, however, is not a single event that occurs in an Executive meeting each month. Rather, preliminary work begins shortly after month's end and continues for some days, involving middle management and others throughout the company (see Figure 4-1 on the next page). They include:

- updating the Sales Forecast;

- reviewing the impact of changes on the Operations Plan, and determining if adequate capacity and material will be available;

- identifying alternatives where problems exist;

- identifying variances to the Business Plan (budget) and potential solutions;

- formulating agreed-upon recommendations for top management regarding overall changes to the plans, and identifying areas of disagreement where consensus is not possible; and

- communicating this information to top management with sufficient time for them to review it prior to the Executive meeting.

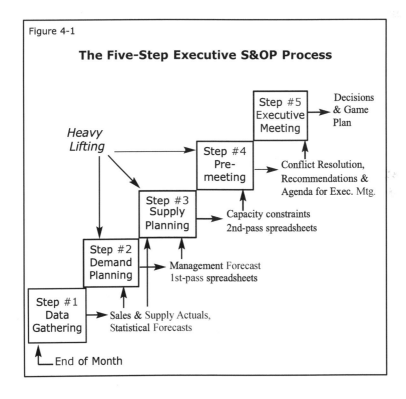

Figure 4-1

The Five-Step Executive S&OP Process

Thanks to the work that's gone before, the monthly Executive meeting should not take a long time – one to two hours is the norm with companies that do this well.

The net result of Executive S&OP for the top management group should be less time in meetings, more productivity in their decision-making processes, enhanced teamwork, and a higher quality of work life. And most of the middle-management people involved in the earlier processes – demand planning, supply planning, Pre-meeting – will experience the same benefits.

Let's take a closer look at each of the steps shown in Figure 4-1.

Step 1 — Data Gathering

Much of this activity occurs shortly after the end of the month. It consists of three elements:

- Updating the files with data from the month just ended – actual sales, production, inventories, and so on.

- Generating information for Sales and Marketing people to use in developing the new forecast. This could include – for volume and, where necessary, mix – sales analysis data, statistical forecast reports, worksheets for field salespeople, and so forth.

- Disseminating this information to the appropriate people.

To make Executive S&OP a timely process overall, it's important that this step be completed within a day or two after the end of the month.

Step 2 — The Demand Planning Phase

This is where people in Sales and Marketing review the information they received from Step 1, analyze and discuss it, and generate the new management volume forecast for the next 15 or more months. Please keep in mind: this forecast must include both existing products *and* new products.

Let's take a look at some of the factors that go into the development of this updated volume forecast:

- Analysis of last month's variances – actual sales to forecast – at a family or subfamily level

- The new statistical forecast, which includes data from the month just ended

- Field sales input regarding customers, particularly large ones

- Market intelligence from trade publications, surveys, input from the field, and so on

- New product plans

- Promotional plans

- Planned price changes

- Competitive activity

- Industry dynamics

• Economic conditions

• Seasonality

• And possibly some others

It's the job of people in Sales and Marketing to use their knowledge of the business to weight these kinds of factors properly. In some industries, historical data and the statistical forecasts could be more important than the input of customers.[1] In other cases, large customers could be the best indicator of the longer-range future.[2]

Involving the folks in Product Development is important here. They typically have the best handle on timing of new product launches; Sales and Marketing should have already made forecasts, and their forecasts should be reviewed for possible changes. The resulting statements of new product demand must be included here so that the Supply Chain people can make the appropriate plans for pre-production samples, line trials, initial build of pipeline inventory, samples, and so forth. These should include new product launches currently underway plus others expected to be launched within the S&OP planning horizon.

---

[1] A word of caution here: If the historical data being used to generate statistical forecasts is shipments to the trade (retailers or distributors), be sure that the point-of-sale (POS) data is not significantly different. It can be quite different, one reason being that some trade customers expand and contract their inventories. In cases such as these, many companies will forecast both demand from the trade and demand from the end consumer to get a clearer picture of what they expect to happen.

[2] Some powerful statistical forecasting routines exist that take into account factors such as economic indicators, consumer attitude, and industry trends. If you're using one of these tools, great; you're a leg up. However, our point here still applies: human judgment by knowledgeable people is central to successful forecasting.

Once the new volume forecast numbers are put together, the job's not quite done. Three things remain:

1. The key assumptions that underlie the forecasts need to be documented. These enable the participants in Executive S&OP to see the assumptions upon which the forecast is based. This can lead to challenges to the forecast, which is certainly a legitimate activity. This in turn gives the forecasters the opportunity to defend the *specifics* of their forecast, rather than having to respond to general comments such as "it's too high."

    A second benefit from documenting assumptions is that, after the period is over, it can be very instructive to review the assumptions and the results and perhaps learn why things didn't work out (or maybe why they did). Learning from one's mistakes is, of course, one of the best ways to get better.

2. Convert the unit volume forecast to dollars based on valid assumptions about revenue conversion. It's critical that the dollar version of the updated volume forecast is viewed and its impact on the business plan is understood before that forecast goes further. People from Finance can be very helpful here; many companies have a Finance person on the Demand Planning team.

3. Lastly, the updated volume forecast needs to be reconciled with the sum of the short-term mix forecasts that are usually developed by the salespeople, with their main focus being the customers. This is sometimes a challenging task, but is essential to assure that everybody is on the same page.

The last step in the Demand Planning phase is to "finalize" the numbers through a senior level demand consensus meeting. This is generally a short meeting of senior level Sales and Marketing people to get their buy-in. Its purpose is to:

- Allow them to ask questions, challenge the numbers, challenge the assumptions, and if need be, change some of them.

- Avoid surprises at the Executive meeting.

- Result in a truly "management-authorized forecast," one that all of the key players have bought into. They've signed off on it. This forecast, then, represents Sales and Marketing's best judgment of future demand volume.

Once this is done, the updated volume forecast is then forwarded to the supply people as an input to Step #3.

Step 3 — The Supply (Capacity) Planning Phase

The newly updated S&OP spreadsheets from Step 2 are the primary input to the Supply Planning phase, which is an Operations responsibility.

Their first step is to modify the Operations Plans for any families or subfamilies that require it. If little or nothing has changed from last month, then there's probably little reason to change anything. On the other hand, changes in the sales forecast, inventory levels, the size of the order backlog, or over/under supply from the prior month can readily trigger a change to the Operations Plan.

These plans then need to be supported by "capacity checks" on the key resources. This requires a conversion of the volume forecasts into a unit of measure appropriate for the respective resource, most often hours. This is done through simplifying assumptions about run rates and mix. These assumptions should be validated each month with data that comes from Step #1.

Often, some degree of sizing or simulation for the amount of anticipated mix variability is necessary. How much of this that can be done is often dependent on the capability of the software that is being used. Simple spreadsheet software affords a certain amount of this capability, but there are more powerful tools available (see Chapter 8).

Outputs from the Supply Planning step are the updated Operations Plans, related Capacity Planning reports,[3] and a list of any supply problems that cannot be resolved or that require decisions further up the ladder. In some cases, demand (as expressed by the forecast) simply exceeds supply by too great a margin; the constraints cannot be overcome within the time allowable. Sometimes these constraints are within the company's production resources; at other times, constraints may exist elsewhere in the supply chain, i.e., outside suppliers.

At other times, acquiring the resources necessary to meet the demand may be feasible but will require spending that can be authorized only by top management. These are the kinds of issues that the supply folks carry into the Pre-meeting, generally with cost/spending data and with margin contribution data provided by

---

[3] These are often the result of a process called Rough-Cut Capacity Planning. They are typically graphical spreadsheets relating *demand* for capacity, derived from the Operations Plan, to the *supply* of capacity at key resources, both in house and at suppliers and contract manufacturers.

the financial participants in both the Demand and Supply Planning phases.

As with Demand Planning, the senior operations executive should serve as a resource to authorize the Supply Plans resulting from this step.

Step 4 — The Pre-meeting

We call this the Pre-meeting because it precedes the Executive session and is preparatory to it. The Pre-meeting's tasks include:

- making decisions regarding the balancing of demand and supply;

- resolving problems and differences so that, where possible, a single set of recommendations can be made to the Executive meeting;

- identifying those areas where agreement cannot be reached, and determining how the situation will be presented in the Executive meeting;

- developing, where appropriate, scenarios showing alternate courses of action to solve a given problem;

- setting the agenda for the Executive meeting.

The key players in this meeting typically include several of the people from the Demand Planning phase, including someone from Product Development, Operations people from the   Supply

Planning step, one or more representatives from Finance, and the Executive S&OP Process Owner – that person or persons who provide overall coordination for the Executive S&OP process.

Their job is to do a review of each product family spreadsheet, including subfamilies where they exist, and to make adjustments where appropriate. They also check for resource constraints, most often using the capacity planning displays cited earlier. Where there are constraints, demand priorities must be established and that, of course, can only be done by Sales and Marketing people.

The outputs from the Pre-meeting include:

• An updated financial view of the business, including matching the latest sales call to the business plan for the total company. (This is typically done on a rolled-up, dollarized spreadsheet covering all families.)

• A recommendation for each product family, contained on a Third-Pass Spreadsheet, as to the future course of action:
  – stay the course, no change
  – increase/decrease the Sales Plan
  – increase/decrease the Operations Plan
  – new product launch issues

• New product launch issues not covered within the product family review.

• A recommendation for each resource requiring a major change: e.g., add people, add a shift, add equipment, offload work to a sister plant, outsource, or reduce the number of people or shifts.

- Areas where a consensus decision could not be reached, possibly as a result of disagreement or where competing alternatives might be "too close to call." In such cases, it can be important for alternative scenarios to be presented – Plan A, Plan B, Plan C – with dollar data as well as units, to show the financial impact.

- Recommendations for changes to demand/supply strategies, where appropriate.

- Agenda for the Executive meeting.

To sum up, the Pre-meeting is a "get-ready" session for the Executive meeting. But it's actually a lot more than that, because the Pre-meeting is a *decision-making* session. The participants decide what to do about issues within their sphere of authority. For other issues, they decide what to recommend to the Executive group.[4] Regarding the latter, the mind-set that the Pre-meeting participants should have is, "If this were our business, what would we decide to do?" Thus it's easy to see why many people look upon the Pre-meeting as an excellent training ground for middle level managers wanting to move into the executive ranks.

Step 5 — The Executive Meeting

This is the culminating event in the monthly Executive S&OP cycle. Its objectives are:

---

[4] At Eli Lilly, they call this the *Compromise Meeting*. In most meetings, some people don't get everything they want; they often have to give a bit in order to settle on a plan that's solid and serves the best interests of the overall business.

- To make decisions on each product family: to accept the recommendation from the Pre-meeting Team or to choose a different course of action.

- To authorize changes in production or procurement rates, where significant costs or other consequences, such as changes to inventory levels or order backlogs are involved.

- To relate the dollarized version of the Executive S&OP information to the Business Plan and where they deviate, decide to adjust the Sales & Operations Plan and/or the Business Plan, as appropriate.

- To "break the ties" for areas where the Pre-meeting Team was unable to reach consensus.

- To review customer service performance, new product issues, special projects, and other issues and make the necessary decisions.

Outputs from the Executive meeting include the meeting minutes, which spell out the decisions that were made; modifications to the Business Plan, if any; and the updated spreadsheets that reflect changes made at the Executive meeting.

All these things taken collectively form the company's authorized game plan. As such, there is urgency to get the word out to all involved people, and for this reason we recommend that the meeting minutes and the spreadsheets be distributed within two working days of the meeting.

FAQ: *What do you do if there's a major event – affecting demand and supply – that occurs shortly after the Executive meeting? It doesn't make sense to wait another whole month to address such a big issue. Is mid-period replanning practical?*

Absolutely. Many successful users, when confronted with such situations, will use an abbreviated, accelerated Executive S&OP process. They'll go through the Pre-meeting steps very quickly, focusing only on those parts of the business that are affected. If the issue can be resolved in one of those steps, fine; mission accomplished.

If not, within a day or two, they'll conduct the Executive meeting – often with a number of the participants on the phone or the Internet – and make the necessary decisions.

Throughout the abbreviated process, they try to keep the steps, the report formats, and the decision-making process the same because the people are familiar with those processes and know they're solid.

In the next chapter, we'll talk about what kinds of companies are using S&OP, and you may be surprised.

Chapter 5

Who's Using Executive S&OP?

Manufacturing companies around the world are using Executive S&OP to help run their businesses better. These companies produce just about everything: consumer packaged goods, production machinery, pharmaceuticals, food, consumer electronics, vehicles, computers, medical equipment, beverages, and on and on. They include:

• large and small companies

• free-standing corporations and divisions of larger enterprises

• suppliers to OEMs (original equipment manufacturers) and those that ship direct to retailers

• manufacturers whose products are made-to-stock, made-to-order, designed-to-order, and finished-to-order – à la Dell Computer.

Best Practice Companies

The book, *Sales & Operations Planning: Best Practices,*[1] tells the stories of 13 highly successful users of Executive S&OP. These organizations are located in the United States, Mexico, Europe, and Australia and their products range from Girl Scout cookies to castings, from Coca-Cola to complex production machinery, from lawn fertilizer to x-ray equipment. Let's look briefly at several of these companies to get a flavor for what real-world companies are doing with Executive S&OP.

[1] John Dougherty and Christopher Gray, *Sales & Operations Planning – Best Practices.* Vancouver, B.C.: Trafford Publishing, 2006.

The Scotts Company – a make-to-stock producer of lawn care products such as Turf Builder, Miracle-Gro, Ortho, Round-Up, and so on. One of the most difficult things for Scotts is that most of their products are fiercely seasonal; in many product families, over 90 percent of the annual volume is sold in less than 90 days. (See Figure 5-1.)

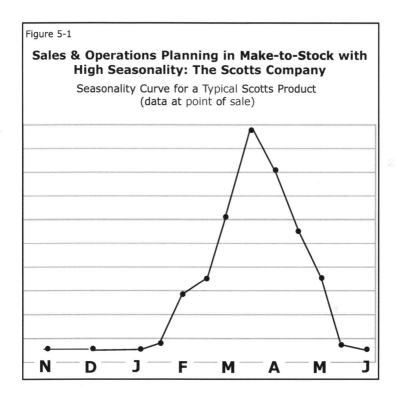

Figure 5-1

Sales & Operations Planning in Make-to-Stock with High Seasonality: The Scotts Company

Seasonality Curve for a Typical Scotts Product
(data at point of sale)

Well, they sure can't produce it all in 90 days; they must start production months ahead of the selling season. Scotts uses Executive S&OP to regulate the beginning of the pre-season build, and subsequently to adjust production rates and mix as they move closer to the season and the demand picture comes into better focus. This has resulted in highly improved customer service levels and far less inventory obsolescence.

Here's Ken Reiff, Vice President of Product Planning: "During the last four years, *almost half of the company's increase in earnings has come from supply chain savings*: inventory down, manufacturing efficiency up, purchase and transportation costs down. All of these are due to improved planning."

Cast-Fab Technologies – a make-to-order foundry and fabrication shop supplying machinery manufacturers. What's one of the toughest parts of their business? Volatile swings in demand for their products: Cast-Fab is at the extreme outer end of the total supply chain and all of the "bull-whip" effects in the earlier stages come home to roost with them.

Their products are sold to companies that make equipment, which is sold to companies making components, which in turn are sold to companies making finished products, which in turn are sold to distributors and retailers, and then to folks like you and us. Sales volumes are very erratic, sometimes increasing or decreasing by 40 or more percent year-to-year. (See Figure 5-2, on the next page.)

President/COO Ross Bushman says: "During 2004, we posted sales increases of over 40 percent, which meant employee call-backs, retraining, new hires, initial training, getting up the learning curve, and so forth. During the same year, we had productivity gains of up to 3 percent![2] We never would have believed this was possible if we hadn't done it. *S&OP played a key role in this*; it gave us the forward visibility to make the right decisions on a timely basis."

---

[2] This company had been using Lean Manufacturing effectively for several years prior to this.

Let's reflect on this productivity gain for just a moment. A 3 percent increase may not sound like much in this age of Lean Manufacturing. However, this company had already implemented Lean successfully. So the 3 percent increase was on top of the gains that came from Lean Manufacturing, not to mention this was achieved during a year where a sizeable amount of new hires could be expected to decrease productivity.

Figure 5-2

Sales & Operations Planning in Make-to-Order with Extreme Cyclicality: Cast-Fab Technologies

	Year-to-Year Sales Change
1993	15% up
1994	38% up
1995	6% *down*
1996	12% *down*
1997	14% up
1998	25% *down*
1999	14% *down*
2000	1% *down*
2001	32% *down*
2002	25% *down*
2003	18% up
2004	46% up

Eli Lilly and Company – primarily a make-to-stock producer of pharmaceuticals and related health-care products. New product development in the pharmaceutical industry is complex and very lengthy, taking a dozen or more years from the initial identification of a potential product to retail sales. Lilly uses their Global S&OP

process to support this challenging and critically important business function. From 2001 through 2005, Lilly introduced ten new products versus an industry average of less than two; Lilly required less than 11 years per product to do these introductions, roughly 25 percent less time than their peers. (See Figure 5-3.)

Figure 5-3

Sales & Operations Planning and New Product Launch: Eli Lilly and Company

New Product Introductions

	Industry Average	Eli Lilly
2001–2005	1.8	10
Years Required	>14	<11

Ron Bohl, one of the key players in their Global S&OP/Supply Chain initiative states: "In the past four years we have launched ten new products and met all demand despite two products that sold significantly above the high-side forecast. Without Global S&OP, we would have been driven to reaction mode, which could have resulted in an increase in investment in new assets, a slow down in our launch plans, and/or missed demand opportunities."

We think these three companies are excellent examples of how businesses use Executive S&OP to enhance their performance in strategically critical areas.

Global Executive S&OP

Another benefit of Executive S&OP was alluded to in the prior section: using the process to help manage global operations. Here's an example of global Executive S&OP from a major multinational company with which we're familiar. The company's global business units are organized by geographic region, called *entities*; each entity has its own Executive S&OP process, using the five-step approach that we outlined in Chapter 4. This supports the entities in taking into account the local cultures, conditions, and operating environments, and in running their own show.

Following each entity's completion of its Executive meeting, the results are sent to the business unit's world headquarters, for consolidation (Figure 5-4, step 6). This creates the global picture of past performance and future outlook.

Last is the global Executive meeting, which is largely financial in orientation. Decisions are made regarding financial matters, of course, but also on occasion addressing the overall demand/supply balance, major inter-entity transfers of production or other resources, new product launch, and so forth. (Figure 5-4, step 7).

Percy Barnevik, formerly the head of the large conglomerate ABB stated, "We are not a global company. We are a collection of companies doing business locally, with intense global coordination." Two issues pop up from that quote:

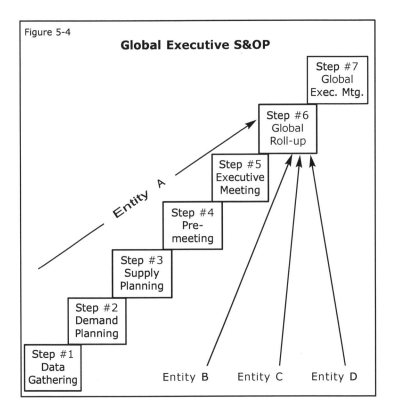

Figure 5-4

Global Executive S&OP

Step #7
Global
Exec. Mtg.

Step #6
Global
Roll-up

Step #5
Executive
Meeting

Step #4
Pre-
meeting

Step #3
Supply
Planning

Step #2
Demand
Planning

Step #1
Data
Gathering

Entity A

Entity B   Entity C   Entity D

- Could ABB use Executive S&OP at the corporate level? Not really, because ABB divisions operate in many different businesses. However, global S&OP could support many of their business units that do business globally. The process shown in Figure 5-4 would occur at the *divisional, business unit* level, not at the corporate level.

- We like Mr. Barnevik's phrase "doing business locally, with intense global coordination." We believe that Executive S&OP supports that intense global coordination and helps it to happen.

Sales & Operations Planning in Non-Manufacturing Environments

We're starting to see Sales & Operations Planning – both Executive S&OP and the mix elements – being used in organizations that don't make things.

Retail

A number of major retailers – The Home Depot, Radio Shack, Coles-Myer in Australia, among others – have active Sales & Operations Planning projects under way or have already implemented the process. Why? Well, the logistics of retailing were simpler when most of the merchandise came from nearby. Today, however, a large volume of products are obtained from half a world away, and this means that the lead times to get product from the source to the store have lengthened a lot.

Furthermore, those lead times now are more variable due to potential transportation delays and disruptions. These companies are finding that Sales & Operations Planning is an effective tool to project demand for months into the future, to harmonize supply with it, and thus to better manage their inventories.

Designer/Distributors

We're using this term to mean companies that design, market, distribute, and sell products – but don't produce them. They use contract manufacturers exclusively. The task here is the same as with company-owned plants: get the supply in sync with demand and provide good forward visibility.

Examples here abound, including many companies who sell electronic equipment. Microsoft also comes to mind; they've been using Executive S&OP for their X-Box business and also for computer hardware such as mouses. Does it really matter who owns the plant that makes the product? Not really; demand and supply still have to be balanced.

Process Design Groups

We are presently working on an Executive S&OP initiative for the central project and process design group within a major chemical company. It's responsible for billions of dollars per year of new plants (design and construction), and new equipment (design and acquisition). Demand comes from the operating divisions – the ones who make and sell products – and this demand can result from new products, growth in existing products, availability of new technologies and so on; it can vary greatly from year to year.

The supply side consists of skilled, highly trained engineers and project management people, and they are not always readily available. Thus the lead times over which demand must be projected can be quite long, so that the supply of the right people can be in place when needed.

The vice president/general manager of this business unit has had prior experience with Executive S&OP during a time when she ran an operating division. She says: "Executive S&OP is a perfect fit to help us balance project demand with the supply of trained people. We need this balance every bit as much as a production operation does."

Does it really matter whether the output of a given organization is a physical product or an "intellectual" product such as design specifications? Not really; demand and supply still have to be balanced.

Banks

A major bank is reporting strong results from Sales & Operations Planning in its consumer loan business. Demand for loans can be variable, based on the season of the year, interest rates, economic conditions, consumer confidence levels, and so on. On the supply side, the processing of loan applications is people intensive: having too many people causes unnecessary costs while not having enough people impacts negatively on customer service, quality, and good will – and may result in lost business. The process helps them to balance the forecasted demand for loans to the supply of people to process them, with the appropriate lead times for hiring and training.

In short, Sales & Operations Planning is spreading into new areas. It's not just for manufacturing companies anymore.

FAQ: *You said that with offshoring, lead times are longer and more variable. I can understand how they're longer, but why are they more variable?*

With offshoring, here's what has to happen after the product (or component) is finished:

1. It gets put in a container and loaded onto a truck.

2. The truck drives to the port where the container is taken off the truck and put on a ship.

3. The ship sails for thousands of miles to reach the port of arrival.

4. The container is taken off the ship and queues up for customs.

5. The container clears customs and is loaded onto a rail car.

6. The rail car travels for hundreds or thousands of miles, and then is put onto a truck.

7. The truck delivers the container to your facility.

Remember Murphy's Law: whatever can go wrong, will go wrong. In the above scenario, there are lots of opportunities for things to go wrong including delays, damage, losing an entire shipment, and so forth. They're all unpredictable and they all add time.

Coming up next are two chapters on implementation: how to make it happen.

Chapter 6

Implementation Part I:
Why the Boss Needs to Be Involved

This chapter and the next cover issues of implementation: how to make it work. Here, we're treating this executive issue separately because it is so vital. This is the most important chapter in the book, aimed squarely at the leader of the business unit: president, managing director, general manager, and so forth. If you have a job like that, or hope to someday, stay tuned.

Over the last 40 years, virtually every new process that has appeared carried with it the following caveat: *top management support is essential.* Some went further: *top management support is not enough; top management commitment is also required.* You may be a bit tired of hearing those kinds of statements by now – even if you recognize their validity.

Executive S&OP is different. Yes, top management support is essential and yes, top management commitment is essential. But that's *not enough,* because Executive S&OP – unlike the others – also requires that the president and his or her staff participate *hands-on in the process.*

In initiatives such as Total Quality/Six Sigma, Just-in-Time/Lean, and others, top management supports, commits, funds, reviews progress, and perhaps participates on occasion. Executive S&OP is different; top management *does it* – each and every month, sometimes more often. They don't do it alone, of course, but they're at the heart of the process: executive decision making.

The First Essential for Success:
Hands-on Participation by the President

Many organizations have tried to implement Executive S&OP but have not been successful, while other companies haven't even tried. Why is that? Well, let's answer that question with another question: what's the most important element of successful Executive S&OP?

Answer: *Executive buy-in, support, leadership, and hands-on participation.*

And another question: what's usually the toughest thing to acquire for an Executive S&OP implementation?

Answer: *Executive buy-in, support, leadership, and hands-on participation.*

To those of us who've been active in this field for a long time, this is not news; here's what we've known for years:

1. A high percentage of users are not satisfied with how well Executive S&OP is working.

2. The major cause of this subpar performance is the lack of hands-on involvement by executives.

Other problems include lack of participation from Sales and Marketing, difficulties in acquiring the data, and little or no tie in to the financial plan. These are serious shortcomings, and they all have one thing in common:

> *Fixing them is far easier if the president is actively*
> *engaged in the Executive S&OP process. When he*
> *or she says, "We are definitely going to make this*
> *work very well; failure is not an option," things*
> *have a way of happening; reluctant people get on*
> *board and momentum begins to build.*

A principle of warfare states: "Hold the high ground." In implementing Executive S&OP, the high ground is the president's office. Once that person is providing the necessary leadership, rapid progress can be made and it will result in a successful implementation.

Still, a question we hear frequently from presidents, general managers, and so forth is: "Do I really need to be involved? We've got good people here; why can't they do it? I'm busy as hell." That's certainly a valid question. The answer of course is that you do need to be involved, and there are three reasons: stewardship, leadership, and the amount of executive time required.

Stewardship

A figure we saw in Chapter 2 is repeated on the next page as Figure 6-1. This shows, for companies not using Executive S&OP, the disconnect that can occur between high level strategic and financial plans on the one hand, and operating level schedules and execution on the other. The executive who complained of "turning knobs not connected to anything" – the leader of a $2 billion business unit – became an S&OP believer following implementation and stated that Executive S&OP "connects the knobs."

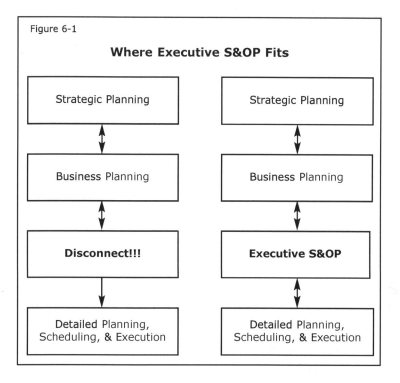

Figure 6-1

Where Executive S&OP Fits

Strategic Planning	Strategic Planning
Business Planning	Business Planning
Disconnect!!!	Executive S&OP
Detailed Planning, Scheduling, & Execution	Detailed Planning, Scheduling, & Execution

As such, Executive S&OP is vitally important, linking detailed schedules and execution to the top level plans, which are of course commitments to some important groups: the corporate office, the stockholders, the financial community, and so forth. The boss –the guy or gal in the corner office – is "on the hook" to deliver those results. Thus, the boss has a stewardship responsibility – first to himself or herself. Equally or more important is the stewardship responsibility to those groups just cited. This responsibility also extends, of course, to other stakeholders: the employees, the suppliers, the community, and so forth. And when the projected results aren't forthcoming, obviously, bad things can happen.

The leader is directly entrusted with the prosperity of the organization and indirectly with that of all the other   stakeholders.

Executive S&OP facilitates the maintenance and expansion of this prosperity, and thus the leader has a stewardship responsibility to use it in the best way possible. He or she *owes it* to the stakeholders. That means hands-on participation.

Leadership

There are three pieces to the leadership element, and the first is being the *tie breaker*. Executives are usually strong-willed people; they've been successful and thus are confident in their abilities. Given that backdrop, let's look at the following scenario:

> Vice President of Sales & Marketing: "Here's our forecast for next year: we're going to sell X million tons of product."

> Vice President of Operations: "Just a minute, John – there's no way you can sell X! The best you could possibly do is to sell Y."

> Vice President of Finance: "I think you're both nuts! We won't sell any more than Z. If we produce to either X or Y, we'll have inventory running out our ears."

So who breaks the tie? The president does. On those occasions, hopefully rare, when the executive staff just can't come to an agreement, it's the president's job to attempt to build consensus and, failing that, to make the call. That call, that decision, then becomes the marching orders for the entire organization.

The second component of the leadership issue is to *set high standards*. The leader has every right to expect work of very high quality, to communicate that expectation, and to hold the participants to that standard. Higher quality processes mean higher quality outputs, whether those outputs are physical products or executive decisions.

The third responsibility of leadership is *to motivate*. When everyone knows that the president is participating, the process will be better. The quality of the preparatory work will be higher, because more care will be given to it.

Further, meeting attendance and participation will be better. Whether I'm an executive, a director, a manager, or perhaps a specialist such as a forecast analyst – if I know that the president is involved in this process, I'll be much more likely to attend those meetings that call for my participation.

Without such leadership by senior management, participation in the Executive S&OP process is often viewed as optional, with the result that over time the process erodes and then goes away – or mutates into a high-level shortage meeting. Participation by the head of the business makes a strong *leadership* statement that Executive S&OP is the process being used to manage these highly important activities: integrating operational and financial planning, balancing demand and supply, and enhancing customer service. This "encourages" other people throughout the organization to do their part in supporting the process.

Executive Time Requirements

Hands-on participation by the president shouldn't be a problem, because so relatively little of his or her time is required. We're talking about one Executive meeting per month lasting between one and two hours.

Many companies have found that this event can often replace several other meetings and thus result in a net reduction in meeting time. For presidents, preparation time is zero. For members of the president's staff, some preparation time may be helpful; this includes authorizing the new sales forecast before it goes to the supply planning step, authorizing the new supply plan before it goes to the Pre-meeting step for demand/supply reconciliation, and so forth.

So how can something so productive require so little time? Well, most of the heavy lifting is done in earlier steps in the process: middle-management people update the forecast and demand plan, identify capacity constraints and raw material problems, and formulate the recommendations to be presented in the Executive meeting.

A group vice president, who had all of his primary divisions operating Executive S&OP successfully, said it succinctly: "Executive S&OP is fiercely efficient. Of all the things I do, it's the most highly leveraged use of my time."

Understanding and Commitment

Regarding a given topic, there are three levels of understanding:

1. Uninformed   2. Semi-informed   3. Fully informed

The degree of understanding interacts with commitment; we need to look at them together. Thus, by linking the two, we have:

1. Uninformed commitment	2. Semi-informed commitment	3. Fully informed commitment

The leader of the business needs to go through the three stages of understanding and their associated levels of commitment in order to provide the leadership necessary for launching the Executive S&OP project and bringing it to a successful conclusion.

Before you picked up this book, you were probably uninformed. If so, you made an uninformed commitment to Executive S&OP by devoting the time to read the book. Upon finishing it, you will be at a semi-informed level of understanding, which may or may not be sufficient to lead you to take the next step: either an Executive Briefing or a 90-day Pilot, both of which are described in the next chapter.

Why do we say "either an Executive Briefing or a 90-day Pilot?" Chalk it up to individual differences. Some executives can read a book – even a short one such as this – and say, "Okay, I've got it. Let's go to the next step." That's making a semi-informed commitment to proceed to the 90-day Pilot. Others need more information, and that can best be achieved through an Executive Briefing.

Following the successful conclusion of the 90-day Pilot, you'll be in a position to make a fully informed commitment to implement the Executive S&OP process across all of the remaining product families. Stay tuned.

FAQ: *You've said that hands-on participation by the president is essential for the process to work properly. But what if the president is called away, and can't attend a given Executive meeting?*

It's simple: reschedule the Executive meeting to a time when he or she can be present.

Two related points:

- We recommend that you schedule all of the monthly Executive meetings a year in advance. That helps the executive group to avoid conflicts with trade shows, corporate events, board of directors meetings, and the like.

- If an executive other than the president is unable to attend an Executive meeting, it's normally not necessary to reschedule. However, that executive needs to designate an alternate to attend the meeting and to be fully empowered to participate in the decision making that will take place.

Chapter 7

Implementation Part II: Putting It All Together

This chapter completes what could be called *Implementation 101.* Chapter 6 focused on executive understanding and buy-in; here we'll look at other important issues.

The ABCs of Implementation

A guy named Oliver Wight – who was a mentor to both of your authors – was the thought leader in this field years ago. One of his insights was to extend the ABC principle[1] to stratify the elements involved in implementing business processes. We've taken what Ollie said and cast it in Executive S&OP terms, as follows:

Working backwards, we'll start with the **C-Item,** the computer hardware and software. It's essential, but it's the item of *least overall significance.* The phrase "necessary but not sufficient" comes to mind.

- This is particularly true with Executive S&OP. Virtually all successful users employ an approach to the processing of S&OP along these lines: import data from the company's data repositories – ERP, CRM, legacy systems – into Excel (or a similar program), where it gets processed, synthesized, and displayed.

---

[1] This is based on Pareto's Law: roughly 20 percent of the items in a group have about 80 percent of the impact. This stratifies the elements within a population by their importance. In customer rankings, for example, the relatively few Class A customers are much more important than the many C customers, which have much lower volume, and the Bs are in the middle. In inventory control, the A items are the few with very high dollar impact and importance, the Bs and Cs less so.

However, this issue can be a show-stopper. If the relatively small amount of systems work required for Executive S&OP is put at the bottom of the systems workload stack, it may take many months for it to work its way up to the top of the stack and get handled.

By that time, momentum for Executive S&OP will probably have evaporated and the project will most likely die. Executive direction, sometimes from the president's office, is usually necessary to place a very high priority on the relatively little systems work required for Executive S&OP, so that it can be completed quickly.

• The **B-Item** is the data – more important than the C-Item and more able to torpedo an Executive S&OP initiative. Included here are sales forecasts, customer orders, finished goods inventories, actual sales and production, and so forth.

In some companies, this issue is relatively easy. In others, particularly in larger organizations, it can be more difficult; the necessary data may reside in many different places with different cut-off dates, different meanings, and so forth. Some of the data may reside in the enterprise software system; some in legacy systems; some in the customer relations management system, and on and on. Sorting out these kinds of issues can take a good bit of effort.

• The **A-Item** is the people. This is the pivotal issue; it's only one-third of the ABCs, but has far more than two-thirds of the impact. Your success with Executive S&OP will hinge largely on the people with regard to two important elements:

1. The people's understanding of what Executive S&OP is, what the benefits are, and their role in the process. We refer to that as *fact transfer.*

2. The people's willingness to change how they do parts of their jobs. We call this *behavior change.*

Enabling Behavior Change

Fact transfer is necessary but not sufficient to accomplish behavior change. Transferring information does not automatically result in people changing their behavior. Here's an example.

Let's pretend for a moment that this is a book about weight loss. It says that, to lose weight, one needs to do three things: 1) eat   less, 2) eat the right stuff, and 3) exercise. Okay, now for a quiz: what are the three things one needs to do to lose weight? Everyone gets the right answer, and fact transfer has been accomplished. But . . . how many of us, after passing that quiz, could proceed to lose weight? Your two authors couldn't, and we suspect that many of you couldn't either. That's because behavior change has not been accomplished.

So, the challenge is to provide the information by which the people can gain this understanding and to provide the leadership to develop their willingness to change. Appendix C lists resources to support this process.

There's good news and bad news here. The good news is that relatively few people will be directly involved with Executive S&OP: in a company of 1,000 employees, no more than two to four dozen people should be directly involved. On the other hand, those few dozen people may face some severe challenges in getting on board.

We believe that people are fundamentally good and that they want to do the right thing. Sure, there are some to whom those words don't apply, but they're a relatively small percentage. Hopefully your organization contains no more of those than the norm, and ideally fewer.

The *corporate culture* often gets in the way of people willingly and enthusiastically changing how they do their jobs. A simple definition of corporate culture is: *how we do things around here*. So, if we want to change the corporate culture, we need to change the way we do things around here. It's that simple.

Next we'd like to explore three aspects of corporate culture that can make it difficult to implement Executive S&OP successfully.

Impediment to Behavior Change #1: Lack of Discipline/Self Discipline

A few years ago, your authors spoke to an executive group of a major manufacturing company. The executives were attentive and engaged as we described the Executive S&OP process and the benefits it could provide. Following the session, however, one of the participants – a guy named Emil – congratulated us on a job well done and then stated, "This S&OP stuff sounds like it could help us a lot. It's too bad we won't be able to make it work."

We were surprised at this of course, and asked, "Why not? You have plenty of bright people, and they seem to be hardworking."

He smiled and said, "Yes, we have all that but what we lack is discipline. This place is dominated by engineers – of which I am one – and they all want to do their own thing. And they do it *when they* want to do it, not when someone else wants it done. When you ask somebody when something will get done, the stock answer is: 'I don't know; you can't schedule creativity.' Further, meetings are considered optional; if they have nothing better to do, they may show up. Or they may not. This behavior exists up and down the line. That's our culture."

Now this was not some Silicon Valley start-up staffed by people with beards, beads, and sandals. This was a successful, old-line manufacturer of large, complex machinery that had been around for almost a century, located on the East Coast. And guess what? Emil was right; they weren't able to make it work. Executive S&OP depends on people doing what they need to do when it needs to be done, or it won't work. In this case, it didn't.

Impediment to Behavior Change #2: Fuzzy Accountability

One of your authors worked on implementing Executive S&OP at an aerospace company. They were okay with the discipline thing, but they struggled with accountability. This company had earned a place in one of those books about the best companies in America to work for, and had a culture that could be described as touchy-feely. This was surprising perhaps for an organization that routinely did business with the likes of Boeing, General Dynamics, Lockheed Martin, NASA, and others not known for sweetness and light. But there it was: accountability in this company was very muted and opaque.

Executive S&OP puts a spotlight on accountability. As a part of the process, performance shortfalls are highlighted and corrective action kicks in. There's good news here: this company worked through their accountability issues and proceeded to use Executive S&OP very well.

Impediment to Behavior Change #3:
Conflict Aversion

A few years ago, one of your authors, Tom, spoke at a conference held at a Midwestern university. Prior to his talk, he was sitting in the back of a meeting room during a session in progress, paying more attention to the notes for his talk that afternoon than to what the speaker, the then-CEO of NCR Corporation, was saying.

Suddenly, one of the speaker's sentences penetrated his consciousness: "At our company, we try hard to get the moose on the table." Tom's head popped up and he said to himself, "What's this with the moose? What in the world is he talking about?" Here's what the speaker was talking about:

- In virtually every company, there are important issues – problems, difficulties, road blocks, and so forth – that are not on the agenda of most meetings.

- Sometimes these are big issues – as big, and often as ugly, as a moose – and they're present in the minds of the people.

- Even though the moose is present in the room, *no one talks about it.* It's taboo.

- Thus, these issues are present in meetings but they're not discussed. And they can be significant impediments to progress.

The speaker went on to say that the challenge is to get the moose on the table – make it impossible to ignore the issue. Raising conflict is good; it's the first step to resolving it.

We believe that success with Executive S&OP comes not only from the proper application of the tools, techniques, and processes but in large measure from the ability to talk about the tough issues. In other words, the ability to get the moose on the table. Not doing so can generate much negative energy and impede progress.

Executive S&OP – done well – often generates conflict, one reason being that it is so cross-functional. This is not a bad thing at all. Rather, as conflict is raised and resolved, the result can be positive energy among the members of the group. See Figure 7-1 on the next page.

Executive S&OP tends to force the moose onto the table. Therefore, organizations that are conflict averse will tend to have a tougher time being highly successful with it. They must learn to:

- Accept differences of opinion as a natural and logical part of the decision-making process.

- Avoid – like the plague – the practice of "shoot the messenger." This is a primary reason why organizations are conflict averse in the first place; people are reluctant to identify and talk about problems for fear that they'll be seen as causing the bad news.

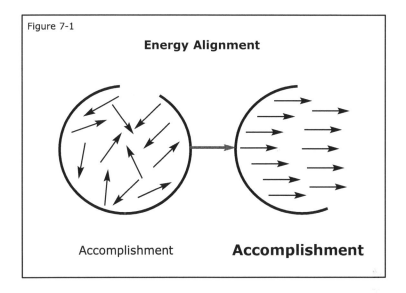

Figure 7-1

Energy Alignment

Accomplishment **Accomplishment**

- Strive for consensus within their groups, being aware that consensus is not the same as unanimity. When a majority of the participants are in agreement, and after all present have been given a chance to air their views, the decision is made and the process moves forward.

When this does not happen, decisions are often avoided; they're simply not made and that in itself is a decision: to do nothing, to maintain the status quo, to sweep problems under the rug. On other occasions, decisions are made at points in the organization not in possession of all the facts, and often these are not good decisions.

A good corporate culture is one that not only accepts the discomfort of raising these issues, but thrives on it without raising negative energy. One of your authors, Bob, takes the principle of getting the moose on the table and puts it into action. For companies with whom he consults, he gives them a stuffed moose to literally be put on the table when a tough issue needs to be addressed. All present are empowered to put the moose on the table, and they do so without fear of becoming the messenger who gets shot.

One last point: this conflict issue can be even more of a challenge in certain countries and cultures where conflict avoidance is the norm and is deeply ingrained in the collective culture. People here may require even more help with confronting problems head on. But it can be done; Global Executive S&OP is operational – and working superbly – all around the world.

Removing Impediments

Certain companies, of course, will have a tougher time than others in dealing with these issues. Some companies have worked through these issues already or perhaps never had them to any degree; others have much to do to remove these kinds of impediments.

But whatever amount of change is needed, it must be led from the top of the organization. This is why the top management element – support, commitment, hands-on involvement – is so important. If people are given the right kind of leadership, then they will begin to understand:

• "Hey, this is a pretty important process and I'm part of it. I need to get my stuff done well and on time, and I need to be present and participate at certain meetings. I can do that."

• "My department's performance against plan is going to be highlighted, but so is every other department's. I can handle that, as long as it's constructive and focuses on things like gaps, root cause, and corrective action – not just on beating people up."

- "I understand that if I don't agree with the way a decision is shaping up, I have the right[2] to present my opposing view and argue in favor of it. If I can sway the group, fine. If not, at least I've had my say and then I'll be able to support the group's decision – even though I may not like it. I remember the Rolling Stones saying: 'You can't always get what you want.'"

If the people have been provided with information, then fact transfer can happen. Next, if the people are getting good signals from the President and his or her staff, then the chances are very good that they'll be willing to get on board, support the Executive S&OP initiative, and change some of the ways they do their jobs.

The Implementation Path

The most successful method for implementing Executive S&OP is the following:

1. *Executive Briefing.* This is an informational business meeting, facilitated by a sure-footed individual with Executive S&OP expertise. This can be someone from within the company – perhaps from a sister division – who has successful Executive S&OP experience, or it could be an outsider with a strong track record of successful implementations.

   The desired outcome of the Executive Briefing is a commitment to the Live Pilot. The Executive Briefing is intended to result in

---

[2] And the obligation, we might add.

a *semi-informed* commitment; the top management group has some knowledge of Executive S&OP, but they haven't experienced it.

2. *Live Pilot.* This step is a limited, low-risk process that takes no more than 90 days, culminating in a Live Pilot on one or two product families. This means actually doing Executive S&OP – the five-step process – for those families.

Low risk and speed are essential. The Live Pilot is intended to demonstrate the benefits of Executive S&OP to the president and his or her staff; its goal is to obtain an *informed* commitment to go to the next step. This is practical because they now know how Executive S&OP works and can see how it can benefit their company. One president, at the conclusion of the Live Pilot, said: "I now have a 'line of sight'; I can see this will benefit us a whole lot."

3. *Expansion and Replication.* Following the Live Pilot, most executive teams feel enthused about the process and are eager to proceed to Expansion and Replication. This brings the remaining product families onto Executive S&OP and typically takes between two and four months, as several families are added each month. Thus this phase easily meets the 90-day criterion.

4. *Integration of Financials.* This involves bringing the financial view into the process, once all product families are on the Executive S&OP process. This step may also include the initiation of unit and dollar simulation, to the extent that the company's software enables it.

For the details of how to implement Executive S&OP, we refer you to *Sales & Operations Planning: The How-To Handbook,* also published by T.F. Wallace & Company.

Implementation Principles

Hold the High Ground. Support, commitment, and hands-on participation by the president and his or her staff are essential. Top management needs to be *engaged.*

People are the A Item. Success with Executive S&OP will hinge almost totally on how well the people – including the executive staff – are informed and enabled to change how they do some aspects of their jobs.

Think Big, Start Small. Follow a low-risk approach, both in dollars and time required. Sometimes the idea of a major project, consuming large amounts of money and people's time, can be a turn off to potentially interested executives. Keep it small and keep it speedy.

Deliver Rapid Value. Visible progress and demonstrated results must be forthcoming within 90 days or less of getting started – and every 90 days or less thereafter. Achieve quick wins and celebrate them.

Keep Your Eyes on the Prize. Don't get sidetracked. Drive towards Executive S&OP. Display the right stuff – the things the executives care about and are measured against.

FAQ: *Can implementation be accelerated by doing the entire Expansion step into one month, instead of two to four months?*

We don't advise it, unless there are very few product families in total. The problem with trying to do it all at once is that it's simply:

- too much work;

- too little time;

- too many things that can go wrong;

- too far to travel up the learning curve.

It's far better to use a phased approach. Taking several more months will result in a safer, more certain implementation.

Coming up next: a look into the future of Executive S&OP. There's good news here.

Chapter 8

A Look into the Future

Here's our prediction about how Executive S&OP will develop over the next half dozen years or so. First, it will continue to grow in popularity because of the following reasons:

- As more and more companies are successful with Executive S&OP, the word gets around. Further, executives from those companies sometimes move to other organizations; they take enthusiasm for the process with them and implement it there.

- As we saw earlier, the Lean Manufacturing community is discovering Executive S&OP and learning that it and Lean work together extremely well. This synergy will become increasingly obvious to many Lean users.

- We'll continue to see more and more uses of Executive S&OP outside of traditional manufacturing.

Second, as more and more supply chains extend around the world, Executive S&OP will increasingly be viewed as essential to harmonize the entire supply chain. It sits at the pivot point, the center of the supply chain, which is where the demand/supply balance needs to occur.

Third, software will play a greater role in Executive S&OP. As complexity and the rate of change increase across the industrial landscape, the need is emerging for S&OP-specific software – particularly its simulation capabilities – to become more powerful, more effective, and more useful to executives and managers. Let's explore this for a moment.

The Top Management War Room

Please use your imagination for just a bit as we peer confidently into the future. We predict that, within a few years, the following kinds of capabilities will be widespread.

Imagine that Executive S&OP is operating successfully in the company of which you're the president. You and your staff are meeting once a month to authorize sales and operations plans that will harmonize demand and supply and to integrate those plans with the financials. In an Executive meeting, while discussing a product family that contains a highly significant new product launch, you raise an issue :

> "I'm getting some input from the field that our competition may be working on a similar product. If they beat us to the market, we'll have just dumped millions of dollars into a 'me-too' product, and that's just not acceptable. If we can move our new product launch up by six weeks, I'm certain we can get to the market first. Can we do that? And, if so, what else might be impacted?"

Your Supply Chain director, Susan Carter, is projecting the S&OP display for this product family onto a large screen from her PC, which contains all of the relevant demand, supply, and financial data. Susan asks for a brief time-out while she runs "what-if" scenarios using your S&OP simulation software. Within a few minutes, she has answers:

- Plan A is feasible and has the lowest cost but it will require getting certain material from a supplier who has had quality and delivery problems in the past – not a good thing for a new product launch.

- Plan B is also feasible and has moderate costs, but will cause some shortages on products 234 and 345.

- Plan C can work and has the lowest total cost, but will cause serious stockouts across much of the product line, because of capacity constraints in Fabrication.

Armed with these facts, you and your staff are well equipped to make the right decision. You may select Plan B: it's feasible; it has only slight negative impact; and it accelerates the new product launch. But there may be more; let's say Carol the CFO raises this question:

> "Now that we've picked Plan B, I have a question. We're moving the new product from next quarter into this quarter. To do that, we're pushing out production of established products into next quarter. I've got to give an earnings projection to Wall Street before long, so what do I tell 'em?"

Susan replies:

> "Carol, here are the deltas on Revenue and Gross Margin between the current plan and Plan B. They don't appear to be major, but you'll probably want to take it into account in developing your earnings call."

The phrase "top management war room" comes to mind. We're looking forward to the day when this type of capability   is widespread: Executive S&OP using simulation software running at the speed of light, allowing rapid development of alternative scenarios; supporting major demand/supply decisions with facts, not guesses; all in a top management setting.

The Running Delta and the Red Zone

There's more. Today, future plans for demand and supply are authorized at the Executive meeting and, shortly thereafter, they begin to change. Why? For any number of reasons:

- Customers change their minds and so schedules have to be shifted. Thus, demand and supply have changed.

- A critical process in the plant goes down, due to an unanticipated machine failure, and schedules have to be shifted. Thus, supply and its related demand have changed.

- A key supplier has a flood, perhaps caused by a hurricane. Everything's up in the air, no pun intended. The demand and supply picture has changed dramatically.

- You decide to accelerate a new product launch. Here also, demand and supply have changed from the last Executive meeting.

Wouldn't it be nice to know how far your current plans have drifted from what you authorized? What's needed is the capability to calculate, again at the speed of light, the difference between: a) the dollars in the volume plans authorized in Executive S&OP and b) the dollarized sum of the detailed schedules currently in place.

We call this the "running delta." Wouldn't it be nice to walk into your office in the morning, hit a few keys on your keyboard, and see the running delta: how closely the current plans are meeting what you and your staff authorized?

Now pretend you're the head financial executive in this business. Every 90 days, you face one of the most difficult parts of your job: making the earnings call to Wall Street, or to corporate so that the CFO can make the call. Within days of the end of the quarter – called the "red zone" – that doesn't sound so difficult. But it can be and often is, because of the factors cited above. The running delta will make red zone calls more valid, more certain, and will facilitate guidance calls made for future quarters.

Audit Trail of Decisions

In some companies, seven-figure decisions are made routinely by people with five-figure incomes. Remember the example of the executive who complained about turning knobs not connected to anything. Seven-figure and sometimes eight-figure decisions were made at the level of detailed scheduling, and not in the president's office. Sales & Operations Planning, including Executive S&OP, helps to minimize this problem.

But even so, wouldn't it be nice to have a system of record – the capability to archive, for each decision of any consequence, who made the decision and why? This would have been a good thing ten and twenty years ago, but today it's even more important in this era of enhanced governance requirements[1] that are being placed on businesses.

---

[1] "Sarbanes-Oxley" in the United States.

Furthermore, for internal purposes, it's often helpful to look back and see *why* we decided to do something; what were the conditions and assumptions underpinning the decision? This is not to point fingers and to affix blame, but rather *to learn* from what we did so that we can do it better next time. As we said earlier, better decision-making processes lead to better decisions. The system of record is part and parcel of better decision-making processes.

*   *   *   *   *

To sum up, industry needs these kinds of capabilities: the top management war room, the running delta, and the system of record. Business is ready for them; and they're now available. Thanks to some superb new simulation software, these kinds of capabilities will become widespread before long. It's no longer a question of "if" but merely "when."

Given this, more attention will be directed toward the financial integration side of Executive S&OP. The use of S&OP-generated financial planning numbers in leading edge users today is quite good, and this practice will become stronger and more widely used in the future. It will play an increasing role in the making of red zone and guidance calls by the CFO. But that's not all.

Adam Szczepanski, one of the CFOs we quoted in the Introduction, has experienced the benefits of successful Executive S&OP in two different companies. Adam had this to say: "This process can do a lot more for the CFO than assisting in making earnings calls. All CFOs should have a strategic financial plan that increases the value of the enterprise. The contribution of Executive S&OP is that it provides formal input on a monthly basis into the strategic direction. It brings life to a strategic process that usually occurs only once or twice per year."

Due to these factors, Executive S&OP will become more visible in the executive suite. It will become widely recognized as an essential element in the top management tool kit, enabling executives and managers to run their companies far better than before.

Thanks for listening. Good luck and God speed.

Appendix A

The Terminology Shift

There's been a terminology shift in this field of balancing demand and supply. Most executives simply won't care about it, but practitioners – especially those who've been close to Sales & Operations Planning – need to get a bit of background on this shift.

Originally, the term *Sales & Operations Planning* referred to an executive-centered decision-making process focusing on *volume* issues. This process utilizes techniques for Demand Planning (forecasting) and Supply (capacity) Planning to accomplish its mission.

However, the meaning of Sales & Operations Planning has broadened. Today, many people view S&OP as dealing with mix in addition to volume. Thus it now can include Master Scheduling and other mix-related tools such as customer order promising, supplier scheduling, plant scheduling, distribution replenishment, and more (sometimes done via the use of Advanced Planning Systems).

Your authors have watched this development, and we endorse it. However, this morphing of the term *Sales & Operations Planning* has generated confusion: people today frequently don't know if a person is talking about the Executive component of S&OP or the detailed mix pieces. Sometimes we wonder if the person using the term knows what he or she means.

So, since Sales & Operations Planning now means more than the executive process, how is the executive process to be identified?

Well, consistent with the principle of keeping it simple, we call it Executive S&OP. Therefore, Sales & Operations Planning – the larger entity – has the following component parts: Executive S&OP, Demand Planning, Supply (capacity) Planning, along with Master Scheduling and related detail-level tools for the managing of mix. (This is shown in Figure 2-2 back on page 20.)

Here's a key point: Executive S&OP is the heart of Sales & Operations Planning; when that critically important piece is missing, much of the power of the total process goes away.

Appendix B

Lean Manufacturing and Executive S&OP: You Need 'Em Both

Authors' note: We wrote this in response to requests for help in explaining the relationship between Lean Manufacturing and Sales & Operations Planning. We patterned it after quality guru Phil Crosby's well-known "elevator speech" of several decades ago.

Lean Manufacturing and Executive S&OP work best when they work together. They do different – and very necessary – things, and you need 'em both.

Lean Manufacturing is a powerful approach whose objective is to eliminate waste, reduce costs, cut lead times, and improve quality, and it does these things superbly. Sales & Operations Planning is a set of forward planning tools to help people balance future demand and supply, and it does this superbly.

Lean is strong on execution; Sales & Operations Planning is strong on decision making for the future.

The scheduling tools within Lean look most closely at the plant and its immediate suppliers. Sales & Operations Planning can extend its future vision out in both directions along the supply chain: to the customers and the suppliers – and in some cases, beyond.

Some of the "leanest" companies in the world use Executive S&OP or variants of it under different names. They do this to balance demand and supply out into the future. Thus the plants and suppliers have good visibility into the future, and are positioned to meet that demand – with material and capacity – effectively and economically.

These companies recognize that "they need 'em both." You probably do too, because they work best when they work together.

Appendix C

Resource Material

Books

Wallace, Thomas F., *Sales & Operations Planning – The How-To Handbook, 2nd Edition.* Cincinnati, OH: T.F. Wallace & Company, 2004.

Wallace, Thomas F. and Robert A. Stahl, *Sales Forecasting: A New Approach.* Cincinnati, OH: T.F. Wallace & Company, 2002.

Wallace, Thomas F. and Robert A. Stahl, *Master Scheduling in the 21st Century.* Cincinnati, OH: T.F. Wallace & Company, 2003.

Wallace, Thomas F. and Robert A.Stahl, *Sales & Operations Planning: The Self-Audit Workbook.* Cincinnati, OH: T.F. Wallace & Company, 2005.

Wallace, Thomas F. and Robert A. Stahl, *Building to Customer Demand.* Cincinnati, OH: T.F. Wallace & Company, 2005.

Dougherty, John and Christopher Gray, *Sales & Operations Planning – Best Practices.* Vancouver, BC: Trafford Publishing, 2006.

Palmatier, George E. and Colleen Crum, *Enterprise Sales & Operations Planning.* Boca Raton, FL: J. Ross Publishing, 2003.

Crum, Colleen and George E. Palmatier, *Demand Management Best Practices: Process, Principles, and Collaboration.* Boca Raton, FL: J. Ross Publishing 2003.

Visual Media

Wallace, Thomas F., *Sales & Operations Planning – A Visual Introduction*. Cincinnati, OH: T.F. Wallace & Company, 2003. (This is a video CD, which contains lectures given by Tom Wallace in conjunction with the Distance Learning Center at Ohio State University. It also contains a separate file of the PowerPoint slides used in the sessions, which companies can use to build their own internal education capabilities.)

Wallace, Thomas F. and Robert A. Stahl, *Building to Customer Demand*. Cincinnati, OH: T.F. Wallace & Company, 2006. (This video CD contains lectures given by Tom and Bob at software company QAD in Santa Barbara, CA.)

Glossary

Abnormal Demand — Unusually large demand and/or demand not in the forecast, frequently from a customer with whom the company has not been doing business.

Aggregate Forecast — See: **Volume Forecast.**

Aligned Resources — Resources that match up very closely with the product families. For example, all of the production for Family A is done in Department 1 and Department 1 makes no product for any other family; similarly for Family B and Department 2, and so on. Determining future capacity requirements for aligned resources is simpler than for matrix resources. See: **Matrix Resources.**

Assemble-to-Order — See: **Finish-to-Order.**

Available-to-Promise (ATP) — The uncommitted portion of a company's current inventory (On-Hand Balance) and future inventory, as expressed by the Master Production Schedule. ATP is an important tool in promising customer orders.

Bias — The amount of forecast error build-up over time, plus or minus. This is a measure of over-forecasting or under-forecasting. See: **Sum of Deviations.**

Build-to-Order — Term popularized by Dell Computer which has a similar meaning to **Finish-to-Order** and **Assemble-to-Order.** See: **Finish-to-Order.**

Business Plan — The financial plan for the business, extending out three to five fiscal years into the future. The first year of the plan is typically the annual budget and is expressed in substantial detail, the future years are less so.

Capable-to-Promise — An advanced form of **Available-to-Promise** (ATP). ATP looks at future production as specified by the master production schedule. Capable-to-Promise goes further; it also looks at what could be produced, out of available material and capacity, even though not formally scheduled. This capability is sometimes found in advanced planning systems (APS).

Capacity Planning — The process of determining how much capacity will be required to produce in the future. Capacity planning can occur at an aggregate level (see **Rough-Cut Capacity Planning**) or at a detailed level. Tools employed for the latter include the traditional **Capacity Requirements Planning** process and the newer Finite Capacity Planning/Scheduling, which not only recognize specific overloads but make recommendations for overcoming them.

Capacity Requirements Planning (CRP) — The process of determining the amount of labor and/or machine resources required to accomplish the tasks of production, and making plans to provide these resources. Open production orders, as well as planned orders in the MRP system, are input to CRP which translates these orders into hours of work by work center by time period. In earlier years, the computer portion of CRP was called infinite loading, a misnomer. This technique is used primarily in complex job shops.

Collaborative Planning, Forecasting, and Replenishment (CPFR) — A process involving participants in the supply chain centering on jointly managed planning and forecasting, with the goal of achieving very high efficiencies in replenishment. CPFR has been referred to as "second generation **Efficient Consumer Response.**"

Deferral — See: **Postponement.**

Demand Management — The functions of sales forecasting, customer order entry, customer order promising, determining distribution center requirements, interplant orders, and service and supply item requirements. **Available-to-Promise** and **Abnormal Demand** control play a large role in effective Demand Management.

Demand Manager — A job function charged with coordinating the **Demand Management** process. Frequently the Demand Manager will operate the statistical forecasting system and work closely with other marketing and salespeople in the Demand Planning phase of Executive S&OP. Other activities for the Demand Manager might include making decisions regarding **Abnormal Demand,** working closely with the Master Scheduler on product availability issues, and being a key player in other aspects of the monthly **Sales & Operations Planning** process. This may or may not be a full-time position.

Demand Plan — The forecast, customer orders, and other anticipated demands such as interplant, export, and samples. See: **Sales Plan.**

Demand/Supply Strategies — In Executive S&OP, these are statements for each product family that define how the company "meets the customer" with that product, its objectives in terms of customer service levels, and targets for finished inventory or order backlog levels. For example, Family A is make-to-stock (i.e., it is shipped to customers from finished goods inventory), its target line fill is 99.5 percent, and its target finished inventory level is ten days' supply.

Demand Time Fence — That period of time in the near future inside of which the unsold forecast is ignored in the **Master Schedule.** In many companies, the Demand Time Fence is set at or near the finishing lead time for the product. The logic is that the unsold forecast can't be produced due to insufficient time and thus should be ignored. See: **Planning Time Fence.**

Design-to-Order — An order fulfillment strategy that calls for detailed design of the product to begin after receipt of the customer order. This is frequently used in companies that make complex, highly-engineered, "one-of-a-kind" products. See: **Finish-to-Order, Make-to-Order, Make-to-Stock.**

Detailed Forecast — See: **Mix Forecast.**

Distribution Requirements Planning (DRP) — A technique that employs the logic of MRP to replenish inventories at remote locations such as distribution centers, consignment inventories, customer warehouses, and so forth. The planned orders created by DRP become input to the **Master Schedule.**

Efficient Consumer Response (ECR) — An approach in which the retailer, distributor, and supplier trading partners work closely together to eliminate excess costs from the supply chain, with the goal of enhancing the efficiency of product introductions, merchandising, promotions, and replenishment.

Exec Meeting — The culminating step in the monthly **Executive S&OP** cycle. It is a decision-making meeting, attended by the president/general manager, his or her staff, and other key individuals.

Executive S&OP — That part of Sales & Operations Planning that balances demand and supply at the aggregate, volume level. It occurs on a monthly cycle and displays information in both units and dollars. Executive S&OP is cross-functional, involving General Management, Sales, Operations, Finance, and Product Development. It occurs at multiple levels within the company, up to and including the executive in charge of the business unit, (e.g., division president, business unit general manager, or CEO of a smaller corporation). Executive S&OP links the company's Strategic Plans and **Business Plan** to its detailed processes — the order entry, **Master Scheduling**, **Plant Scheduling,** and purchasing tools it uses to run the business on a week-to-week, day-to-day, and hour-to-hour basis. Used properly, Executive S&OP enables the company's managers to view the business holistically and provides them with a window into the future.

Family — See: **Product Family.**

Financial Interface — A process of tying financial information and operating information together. It is the process by which businesses are able to operate with one and only one set of numbers, rather than using data in operational functions that differ from that used in the financial side of the business.

Financial Planning — The process of developing dollarized projections for revenues, costs, cash flow, other asset changes, and so forth.

Finish-to-Order — An order fulfillment strategy where the customer order is completed shortly after receipt. The key components used in the finishing or final assembly process are planned and possibly stocked based on sales forecasts. Receipt of a customer order initiates the finishing of the customized product. This strategy is useful where a large number of end products, most often due to a high degree of optionality within the product, can be finished quickly from available components. Syn: **Assemble-to-Order, Build-to-Order.**

Forecast — See: **Sales Forecast.**

Forecast Consumption — The process of replacing uncertain future demand (the forecast) with known future demand (primarily customer orders).

Forecast Error — The amount that the forecast deviates from actual sales. Measures of forecast error include **Mean Absolute Deviation** (MAD) and **Sum of Deviations** (SOD). See: **Variability.**

Forecast Frequency — How often the forecast is fully reviewed and updated, most commonly monthly.

Forecast Horizon — The amount of time into the future that the forecast covers.

Forecast Interval — The size or "width" of the time period being forecasted. The most commonly used intervals are weekly or monthly.

Kanban — A method used in **Lean Manufacturing** in which consuming (downstream) operations pull from feeding (upstream) operations. Feeding operations are authorized to produce only after receiving a Kanban card (or other trigger) from the consuming operation. In Japanese, loosely translated it means card or signal. Syn: **demand pull**.

Lean Manufacturing — A powerful approach to production that emphasizes the minimization of the amount of all the resources (including time) used in the various activities of the enterprise. It involves identifying and eliminating non-value-adding activities in design, production, **Supply Chain Management,** and customer relations.

Line Fill Rate — The percentage of order lines shipped on time and complete. See: **Order Fill Rate.**

Make-to-Order — An order fulfillment strategy where the product is made after receipt of a customer's order. The final product is usually a combination of standard items and items custom designed to meet the requirements called out in the customer order. See: **Design-to-Order, Finish-to-Order, Make-to-Stock.**

Make-to-Stock — An order fulfillment strategy where products are finished before receipt of customer orders. Customer orders are typically filled from existing finished goods inventory. See: **Design-to-Order, Finish-to-Order, Make-to-Order.**

Master Schedule — The tool that balances demand and supply at the product level, as opposed to **Executive S&OP,** which balances demand and supply at the aggregated **Product Family** level. It is the source of customer order promising, via its **Available-to-Promise** capability, and contains the anticipated build schedule for the plant(s) in the form of the **Master Production Schedule.**

Master Scheduling Policy — A document authorized by top management that defines roles and responsibilities. It directs the Master Scheduler and others on both the demand and supply sides of the business regarding who owes what to whom. It spells out who is empowered to make decisions under what circumstances and in which time zones.

Material Requirements Planning (MRP) — A set of techniques that uses bills of material, inventory data, and the **Master Production Schedule** to calculate requirements for materials. It makes recommendations to release replenishment orders. Further, since it is time phased, it makes recommendations to reschedule open orders when due dates of orders (supply) and need dates (demand) are not in phase.

Matrix Resources — Resources that do not match up with the product families. For example, Department 1 makes products in Families A, C, D, and G. Determining future capacity requirements for matrix resources is more complex than for aligned resources. See: **Aligned Resources.**

Mix — The details. Individual products, customer orders, pieces of equipment, as opposed to aggregate groupings. See: **Volume.**

Mix Forecast — A forecast by individual products. Sometimes called the detailed forecast. It is used for short-term scheduling for plants and suppliers (and may be required for certain long lead time, unique purchased items).

Operations Plan — The agreed-upon rates and volumes of production or procurement to support the **Sales Plan (Demand Plan, Sales Forecast)** and to reach the inventory or order backlog targets. The Production Plan, upon authorization at the **Exec Meeting,** becomes the "marching orders" for the Master Scheduler, who must set the **Master Production Schedule** in congruence with the Production Plan. Syn: **Production Plan.**

Order Fill Rate — The percentage of customer orders shipped on time and complete as opposed to the total number of orders. Order fill is a more stringent measure of customer delivery performance than line fill. For example, if only one item out of twenty on a customer order is unavailable, then that order counts for zero in the order fill calculation. The line fill percentage in this example would be 95 percent. See: **Line Fill Rate.**

Planning Time Fence (PTF) — The period of time inside of which detailed planning must be present in the **Master Schedule.** Normally, the Planning Time Fence approximates the cumulative lead time of the product plus 25 to 50 percent. Sometimes called the Critical Time Fence. Most Master Scheduling software will not alter the **Master Production Schedule** within the PTF, only outside of it.

Plant Scheduling — The process of creating the detailed schedules needed by the plant(s). Plant schedules can include the finishing schedules, fabrication schedules, and so forth.

Postponement — An approach that calls for waiting to add options into the product until after the customer order is received and then finishing the product very quickly.

Pre-meeting — The preliminary session prior to the **Exec Meeting** in **Executive S&OP.** In it, key people from Sales & Marketing, Operations,

Finance, and New Product Development come together to develop the recommendations to be made at the Executive session.

Product Family — The basic planning element for **Executive S&OP**; its focus is on families and subfamilies (volume), not individual items (mix).

Product Subfamily — A planning element sometimes used in S&OP that provides a more detailed view than product families, but not at the extreme detail of individual products. Product Family A, for example, might contain three subfamilies — A1, A2, A3 — and each of those might contain a dozen or so individual products. See: **Product Family.**

Production Plan — See: Operations Plan.

Projected Available Balance — The inventory balance projected out into the future. It is the running sum of on-hand inventory, minus requirements, plus scheduled receipts and (usually) planned orders.

Resource — Those things that add value to products in their production and/or delivery.

Rough-Cut Capacity Planning — The process by which the **Operations Plan** or the **Master Production Schedule** can be converted into future capacity requirements. Frequently the Operations Plan, expressed in units of product, is "translated" into standard hours of workload (which is a common unit of measure for production operations). Rough-Cut Capacity Planning can be used at the departmental level, or for subsets of departments, down to individual pieces of equipment or specific skill levels for production associates. This process can also be carried out for suppliers, for warehouse space, and for non-production operations such as product design and drafting.

Running Sum of Forecast Error (RSFE) — See: **Sum of Deviations.**

Sales & Operations Planning (S&OP) — A set of business processes that helps companies keep demand and supply in balance. It includes **Executive**

S&OP, Sales Forecasting and Demand Management, Rough-Cut Capacity Planning, Master Scheduling and other detailed scheduling tools for both plants and suppliers. Originally used to identify only aggregate planning (as in Executive S&OP), its meaning has expanded to include also those elements that operate at the detailed, mix level.

Sales Forecast — A projection of estimated future demand.

Sales Plan — The details backing up the **Sales Forecast.** It represents Sales & Marketing management's commitment to take all reasonable steps necessary to achieve the forecasted level of actual customer orders.

SOD — See: **Sum of Deviations.**

Stockkeeping Unit (SKU) — An individual finished product. In the more rigorous use of the term, it refers to a specific, individual product in a given location. Thus, product #1234 at the Los Angeles warehouse is a different SKU from the same product at the Chicago warehouse.

Subfamily — See: **Product Subfamily.**

Sum of Deviations (SOD) — The cumulative sum of forecast error (plus or minus) over time. As such, it is a measure of bias. Also called **Running Sum of Forecast Error (RSFE).**

Supplier Scheduling — A purchasing approach that provides suppliers with schedules rather than individual hard copy purchase orders. Normally a supplier scheduling system will include a contract and a daily or weekly schedule for each participating supplier extending for some time into the future. Syn: Vendor Scheduling**.**

Supply Chain — The organizations and processes involved from the initial raw materials through manufacturing and distribution to the ultimate acquisition of the finished product by the end consumer.
ABB, 56

Supply Chain Management — The planning, organizing, and controlling of supply chain activities. This can include suppliers, suppliers' suppliers, customers, customers' customers, end consumers, transportation providers, and so on.

Supply Planning — The function of setting planned rates of production (both in-house and outsourced) to satisfy the **Demand Plan** and to meet inventory and order backlog targets. Frequently, **Rough-Cut Capacity Planning** is used to support this.

Time Fence — A point in the future that delineates one time zone from another.

Vendor Managed Inventories —— A process that places the replenishment decision-making in the hands of the supplier. It's the supplier's job to ensure that the customer does not run out of stock and to keep the inventories at the agreed-upon levels.

Volume — The big picture. Sales and production rates for aggregate groupings — product families, production departments, etc. — as opposed to individual products, customer orders, and work centers. See: **Mix.**

Volume Forecast — A forecast by product groupings such as families, classes, and so forth. Also called the aggregate forecast or the product group forecast, it is used for sales planning, for **capacity planning** at the plants and suppliers, and for financial analyses and projections.

Index